Skills for Excellence

To

Anita, Oscar & family, and Bita

Skills for Excellence

by

Luis S. R. Vas

Innovativeness • Thinking Skills • Problem Solving Abilities • Creativity • Intuition • Personality • Time Management • Learning Ability • Communication Skills • Memory • Health & Fitness

PUSTAK MAHAL®

Administrative office and sale centre

J-3/16 , Daryaganj, New Delhi-110002
☎ 23276539, 23272783, 23272784 • *Fax:* 011-23260518
E-mail: info@pustakmahal.com • *Website:* www.pustakmahal.com

Branches
Bengaluru: ☎ 080-22234025 • *Telefax:* 080-22240209
E-mail: pustakmahalblr@gmail.com
Mumbai: ☎ 022-22010941, 022-22053387
E-mail: unicornbooksmumbai@gmail.com

ISBN 978-81-223-0073-4

Printed at : **Radha Offset, Delhi**

Preface

Almost day by day the world grows more competitive. More businesses compete for the same markets. As technologies develop, companies are able to achieve better quality in products and processes as well as greater productivity. As customers demand better quality from companies, so also companies demand excellence from their employees. After Total Quality Management, companies have been after Total Quality People. That is another term for excellence.

How do you achieve excellence in a world of growing complexity and rapid technological change? The first step is a thirst for excellence. This is the motivation to achieve quality in whatever you do. Around the world numerous consultants have combined insights from behavioural sciences to train people in achieving excellence in various realms. But excellence requires specific skills in various areas.

In **Skills for Excellence** I have tried to bring together within one volume most of the ideas and practices which are being taught in enterprises around the world. I have started with achievement motivation and shown how, as research has proved, this skill can be cultivated and developed. The other skills presented in this book are innovativeness drawn from the ideas of Peter Drucker and others; thinking skills from the concepts developed by Edward de Bono; a problem solving technique devised by Rudolf Flesch; creativity as taught by Robert Fritz.

Excellence is not only a matter of rational thinking. Much depends upon the use you make of your intuition. I have presented here techniques to awaken and expand your intuitive powers. Your personality, too, is an important factor in your success in achieving excellence in your work and relationships. I have presented two approaches to personality and how it can be developed: Typewatching and the Enneagram. They have proved useful in training courses worldwide.

There are apparently simpler skills, too, that you should not neglect and which may prove crucial in your work and life. They are: time management, learning ability, communication skills and your retention powers. An equally basic but often neglected skill is the ability to maintain your health and fitness.

All these skills have been covered at length in the specific chapters related to them. In them, too, I have adapted ideas from masters in their respective fields.

I hope these techniques will prove useful to you as you seek excellence in your career and life. I shall be grateful for any feedback you can give me based on your experiences with them. Please write to me at the address below:

Luis S. R. Vas
Human Potential Institute
203-C, La Chapelle, Evershine Nagar,
Malad (W)
Mumbai-400 064.
India

CONTENTS

1

The Secret of Achievement

Narayanan was a 37-year-old man from Kakinada, A.P. He enjoyed high social status in his town because he was the son of a prominent landlord. He lived with his aged and ailing father, mother, wife, three children, two younger brothers and three unmarried teen-age sisters in a large house. He was engaged full time in the management of several charitable institutions run by the family for several generations.

But he felt vaguely dissatisfied with life. One day he heard about a ten-day course on achievement motivation offered by a training institute in Hyderabad and decided to enroll. At the end of it Narayanan decided to change the direction of his life drastically by going into manufacturing though neither he nor anyone in his family, then or earlier, had had any experience in running a business. He acquired an industrial firm investing a large sum of money modernising it, after convincing his mother and sisters to give him a loan from the joint family funds. When the venture proved successful, he joined hands with a partner to launch another project, a large graphite processing plant.

The course which Narayanan successfully completed was based on the following psychological propositions, which were demonstrated to be true from the effect the course had on the lives of most of the participants.

1. The more reasons an individual has to believe that he can, will or should develop an achievement motive, the more the educational attempts designed to develop that motive are likely to succeed.
2. The more an individual commits himself to achieving concrete goals in life related to the newly formed motive, the more the motive is likely to influence his future thoughts and actions.
3. The more an individual keeps a record of his progress towards achieving goals to which he is committed, the more the newly formed motive is likely to influence his future thoughts and actions. (Source: Motivating Economic Achievement, David McClelland and David Winter).

The following exercises are based on the foregoing propositions and are designed to promote goal achievement in people of various kinds of background.

Overcome Barriers to Achievement

Purpose : To help you assess and overcome barriers to achievement.

Duration : Unlimited, but can be done in 10-minute segments.

Procedure

Three of the most serious barriers to success are fear of success, fear of failure, and perfectionism. To determine if your career may be hampered by these, take the following test. Be honest with yourself. Do not try to guess how a successful person might respond.

My Attitudes and Feelings. Rate your reactions as A, B, C, where:

A = Agree
B = In-Between or Don't Know
C = Disagree

1. When things seem to be going really well for me, I get uneasy because I know it won't last.
2. Most of the time I find that I measure up to the standards I've set for myself.
3. I find it difficult to tell my friends that I excel at something.
4. It is important for me to be liked by people with positions of higher status and power than mine.
5. When I win a competitive game, I feel a little sorry for the other player.
6. When I have to ask others for help, I feel I'm imposing on them.
7. Although I may experience occasional difficulty doing so, I generally finish essential projects.
8. When I think I've been too forceful in making a point to a colleague, I get worried that I might have made him feel unfriendly towards me.
9. When colleagues compliment me on my work, I feel they are being insincere.
10. When I complete an important piece of work, I am usually satisfied with the result.
11. When engaged in competitive games, I make more mistakes near the end than at the beginning.
12. When my boss praises my work I wonder whether I can live up to his expectations in the future.
13. At times I believe I have got as far in my career because of good luck, not because I deserve it.

14. It is just as important to win a game as to merely enjoy it.
15. I often daydream about accomplishing something that no one else has ever accomplished before.
16. I like being the centre of attention in a social gathering.
17. Most of my colleagues are secretly pleased when I get into trouble.
18. I'm pretty skillful at most things I try.
19. When I make a decision, I usually stick to it.
20. I often get excited when I start working on a new project, but it gets stale rather quickly.
21. I often feel let down after completing an important project.
22. At times my accomplishments amaze me because I feel that I rarely put in the effort that I could.
23. When I hear about the accomplishments of others, I tend to think how little I myself have accomplished.
24. I'm not influenced one way or another by persuasive people.
25. When a project seems to be going well, I often get scared that I'll do something to botch it.
26. The surest way to get disappointed is to want something too much.
27. I seldom consult my associates before deciding to go ahead with a project.
28. When I decide to go after something, I usually get it.
29. Before I decide what procedures to use in my work, I like to ask my colleagues for advice.
30. I sometimes downgrade my abilities so others won't expect too much from me.
31. When someone I know succeeds at something, I often feel I could have done as well, or better.

32. I don't mind having to ask others for help.
33. I seldom participate in competitive games.
34. When I have to complete an important project in a hurry, I get so upset that I can't concentrate on it.
35. I feel most of the time that I do things as well as I can.
36. I prefer to settle for less than I want rather than get into an argument about it.
37. I dislike people who look out for themselves first.
38. When I commit myself to something, I go through with it.
39. I can easily concentrate on a task for a long period of time.
40. Often, when I sit down to solve a problem, I get distracted and my thoughts drift off to other things.
41. My work tends to pile up so much that I have difficulty completing all of it.
42. I have little trouble saying no to people.
43. I like to explore subject areas in which I have little knowledge.
44. I have what it takes to be a success in my chosen field.
45. While developing a new idea I often tend to get stuck at a certain point.
46. I like to avoid situations where there could be potential conflict.
47. Even when I have good ideas, I frequently don't follow through on them.
48. I don't mind working on difficult problems, even when I'm not sure I can figure them out.
49. When I'm in a heated discussion, my mind often goes blank.
50. When starting to work on an important project, I often find many other things that should be taken care of first.

Scoring Instructions

To get your score for the test, circle and add up the values for items 1 through 25. Then add up a separate score for items 26 through 50.

Items	Answers		
	A	B	C
1.	–1	0	2
2.	2	0	–1
3.	–1	0	1
4.	–1	0	1
5.	1	0	–1
6.	–2	1	2
7.	3	0	–2
8.	–2	1	2
9.	–1	0	1
10.	2	0	–1
11.	–2	0	2
12.	–2	0	2
13.	–2	1	2
14.	2	1	–1
15.	3	0	–2
16.	2	1	–1
17.	–1	0	1
18.	2	1	–1
19.	3	0	–2
20.	–2	1	2
21.	–1	0	1
22.	–1	0	1
23.	–2	0	2
24.	3	1	–2
25.	–1	0	2
26.	–2	1	2
27.	1	0	–1
28.	3	1	–2
29.	–1	0	1

Contd...

Continued

Items	Answers		
	A	B	C
30.	–2	0	2
31.	3	0	–2
32.	2	1	–1
33.	–2	1	2
34.	–2	0	2
35.	2	1	–1
36.	–2	0	2
37.	–2	1	2
38.	3	0	–3
39.	2	0	–2
40.	–2	0	2
41.	0	1	2
42.	2	1	–1
43.	3	0	–2
44.	3	0	–2
45.	–1	0	1
46.	–2	0	1
47.	–2	0	2
48.	3	0	–2
49.	–3	0	3
50.	–3	0	3

What Your Score Means

A score of 28 to 47 on questions 1 through 25 indicates that you have no problem with "fear of success". You are strongly achievement oriented. You like to come up a winner. You are able to make commitments and preserve with your projects until a successful outcome is assured. You take pride in your skills and talents and you have full confidence in yourself. Although independent-minded and assertive, your relationships with others are trustful and open.

If you scored 4 to 27, you have a tendency to occasionally pursue unrealistically high standards, and you're not always satisfied with your achievements. You prefer win/win rather than win/lose situations. You're concerned about what others think of you and you want to be liked by everybody. Because of a fluctuating self-esteem, you periodically lapse into self-critical ruminations about your abilities to succeed. You have some trouble making decisions and then sticking to them. The limelight is certainly not for you, and you regard those who want to be the "life of the party" with scorn. Because you have moderate fear of success, you're not fully using your success potential.

A score of-25 to 3 indicates that you want to win, but frequently lose in the end. You tend to be overly passive and withdrawn, and prefer to take the back seat in competitive situations. Because of your excessive need to be liked, you refrain from arguments and contests of will. You lack full self-confidence and you seldom give yourself the credit you deserve for your accomplishments. You tend to be somewhat distrustful of other people's motives and feel that human nature cannot always be relied upon. Fear of success definitely hampers your accomplishments.

A score of –36 to –24 means that "fear of success" is a definite problem for you. You're very non-assertive and self-effacing and consider modesty a virtue. You're never satisfied with your achievements and frequently manage to snatch defeat from victory. Doubtful about whether you've any luck at all, you tend to worry about the future most of the time. Because you're too concerned about others' opinions of you, you frequently act like a "doormat", although you don't like it one bit. You like neither to give, nor to receive compliments.

Second Half of Test

A score of 35 to 54 on questions 26 through 50 indicates that you're seldom preoccupied with the possibility of failure. Rather, you move towards your objectives with a sure feeling of confidence and act as if it was impossible for you to fail. You have the ability to stick to difficult tasks and problems and you seldom give up You seldom compare your achievements with others, but if you do, you almost always feel you could have done better than they did. Attributes of self-reliance and self-trust enable you to remain imperturbable in many challenging situations. You're able to maintain continuous drive and a high level of thrust in whatever you do.

If you scored 8 to 34 on questions 26 through 50, you're occasionally hampered by an overly cautious and hesitant attitude towards your objectives. Frequently you even entertain serious doubts about reaching the goals you've set for yourself. You have trouble concentrating when something important is at stake. Before you act on your ideas, you feel compelled to enlist other colleagues' opinions and evaluations of your plans. If they don't approve or encourage you, you frequently give up on your plans.

A score of-25 to 8 indicates a marked fear of failure in many areas. You lack self-trust and have an unrealistically low image of yourself. You tend to avoid important tasks and busy yourself with the tried and tested. Competitive situations are anathema for you, as well as being with people you don't know. In meetings you feel that everyone else has more witty and knowledgeable things to say than you do, and you tend to generally act in a timid and embarrassed way. Because of your fear of failure, your aspirations are low and you hesitate to take any kind of risks.

If you scored –47 to –24, you show complete lack of self-confidence and you're constantly worried about your capabilities. You avoid any and all challenges and prefer to stick to routine, familiar tasks. With other people you seek timid accommodation and dislike colleagues who show boisterous self-assertion. Because you fear failure so much, you have anti-success attitudes and feel that those who climb the ladder of success will find upon reaching the top that isn't resting on anything.

Fear of Success

There are individuals who have a basic ambivalence about succeeding: they want but also want *not* to succeed.

While those who have a marked fear of failure prefer to retreat from competitive situations, and from the risks involved in trying to improve their career prospects, success-fearing individuals welcome success-oriented activities. Many of them are exceedingly ambitious and desire to be recognized for their achievements. But as soon as they've made any significant progress toward a desired objective, they feel a compulsion to check themselves and to find ways to sabotage success.

Development

To better understand the dynamics of the fear of success, let's take a look at how it develops.

Most success-fearing people internalize society's mixed-up attitudes toward success early in life. On the one hand, society extolls the competitive and individualistic spirit. Those who succeed are admired for their competence, talent, courage, enterprise and other positive attributes. Those who fail are viewed with contempt or pity. Individuals supposedly fail because they are incompetent or lazy. On the other hand, there is a cultural admonition that nice people should be modest, self-effacing, unselfish, and giving. Success is associated with greed and is looked upon as something immoral or even contemptible. It has become fashionable, of late, to be cynical about success and to sneer at ambition. As a result, many are anxious to project an organisational self of a harmless nonentity.

Childhood's Impact

These paradoxical and conflicting attitudes toward success were transmitted through their parents and older siblings. In addition, there is also a distinctive home atmosphere that seems to foster the development of the fear-of-success syndrome. Success-fearing people were invariably reared in homes where high standards of success and competition were encouraged and valued. At the same time, however, they were discouraged, or even punished, if they were too competitive or if they showed any overt pleasure in winning. The parents of success-fearing individuals gave them confusing signals about success and winning, and were highly intrusive and controlling in their interactions with them. Many of these parents also expressed to them a painful conflict. Consciously they are anxious to succeed, but their subconscious fears and inhibitions about succeeding are activated soon after they've embarked on the path to success.

Second, fear of success persists in their adult lives because of their suppressed childhood experiences. Most success-fearing people cannot justify their behaviour rationally because of any experience of negative success-consequences in their adult years. There simply haven't been any they can point to. But they continue to maintain their irrational fear of success in spite of any objective evidence to the contrary. The childhood tapes are still being played over and over in their subconscious.

Third, success-fearing people use a variety of defence mechanisms and rationalizations to protect them from the intense anxiety created both by their initial self-enhancing drives and later self-defeating maneuvres. One of the mechanisms they use is projection of the motives to succeed to external, situational requirements. Another one is a denial of any internal desire to succeed. When, at times, they are successful in spite of themselves, they tend to attribute it to luck, or to others' help, or stupidity, rather than to their own abilities and efforts. If this doesn't sound plausible, they tend to say that the accomplishment was easy. By playing down and repudiating their own competence, they manage, in addition, to rob themselves of any real enjoyment of the achievements they do attain.

Fear of Failure

Another category of people who do not give themselves full permission to succeed are the failure-fearers. Many people are held back from using their full potential because of their lack of faith in their ability to succeed. To be sure, some people claim they have the needed self-confidence to succeed and that the prospect of failure doesn't bother them, but this is mere lip-service. When asked why they haven't started to pursue an important pet project, they respond with all kinds of excuses or complaints about the obstacles and difficulties that stand in the way: too little time, pressing other obligations, lack of resources, corporate restrictions, and so on.

People with marked fear of failure tend either to set for themselves easy to reach, modest goals, or, in the other extreme, they pursue goals that are so difficult and way out that no one could blame them if they failed to reach them. Some people hide their deep sense of inadequacy behind a high self-aggrandizing image of themselves. They develop all kinds of grandiose and unrealistic plans, pursue them by fits and starts, and when it finally dawns on them that they're pursuing the impossible, their sense of failure and inadequacy breaks through their self-protective armour of grandiosity.

Withdrawal

Most failure-fearing people, however, tend to withdraw from competition and risk-taking. They are the underachievers who look for safe little niches and innocuous tasks that pose little or no threat of failure. Performance risk of failure has to be avoided at all costs because it would expose their inadequacies to their bosses and peers. The safer course to take is to remain modest and inconspicuous. Failure-fearers' phobic reaction to competitive situations is due to their fear of humiliation and contempt, which to them represent failure's reward. Because failure-fearing people have extremely low levels of aspiration, they often appear indolent and passive. Because of their general unwillingness to act, and their tendency to shun risks and avoid responsibilities, these unfortunate people suffer great personal impoverishment and almost a total negation of their potential. Eventually many of them fall prey to depressive moods and deep feelings of helplessness.

Unrealistic

Even those people who are not plagued by exaggerated self-doubts and thoughts of failure tend to be somewhat unrealistic in their estimation of themselves and of the challenges they face. They usually over-estimate the difficulties and underestimate their own abilities for resolving them. As a result, they make only half-hearted efforts when pursuing desired objectives. Underestimation of potential is largely responsible for the vacillation and excessive caution people show when commitment to a goal is called for. Hesitation and caution are not, in themselves, bad, but if continued over a period of time, they have the propensity to strengthen negative projections of outcome, which can snowball into a self-fulfilling prophecy of failure.

Risk Taking

Failures, mistakes, setbacks are an integral part of achieving success. It is doubtful that any one ever really succeeded without taking risks. And risks inevitably entail some failure experiences. In the final analysis, what counts is not our mistakes and failures, but our emotional willingness to risk and accept failure. Strange as it may seem, when we have the courage to risk personal rejection, wasted effort, and even psychological defeat should our efforts fail, we've taken a giant step toward liberating ourselves from the fear of failure. And once we are free of this fear, there is almost an immediate upsurge of energies to exercise our capacities. Frequently we discover capacities we didn't even know we had, and that far exceed our expectations. Freed from the fear of failure, we're not only free to do our best, but to discover what its farthest reaches may entail.

Perfectionism

Another serious barrier to the attainment of success is perfectionism. Perfectionists invariably set for themselves exceedingly high standards and overambitious goals. They feel that if they don't aim high, they would remain just average or medicore. Perfectionism is the price they have to pay to reach noteworthy levels of excellence.

To be sure, there is such a thing as a healthy pursuit of excellence, and many are able to derive genuine satisfaction from their efforts to reach high standards. Perfectionists' pursuit of excellence, however, is unhealthy. First, their standards are completely unrealistic and set way beyond reach or reason. Second, they are driven and compulsive, always pursuing and reaching for impossible goals. Third, they never really enjoy any of their achievements. Every objective they reach falls short of what was in their mind's eye and they feel disappointed.

Black or White

The chief reason why perfectionists tend to experience more punishment than reward from their attainments is that they habitually think in all-or-nothing or black-and-white terms, with no gradations of gray in-between. Even a minor short-fall provides for them an occasion for wounding self-criticism. Fourth, since their sense of self-worth is inextricably linked to high accomplishment, it stands on very shaky ground.

Reaching for the stars exacts an enormous toll. Perfectionists have been found to suffer from chronically low self-esteem, constant performance anxiety and depressive moods. As a result, their productivity is either inhibited or intermittent. Their mood disorders and relentless self-doubts also adversely affect their self-control and their interpersonal relationships. Preoccupation with impending failure, or inability to measure up to exacting standards, doesn't leave much room for friendly give-and-take with others.

'Type A' Persons

Perfectionists closely resemble that Type-A personality described years ago by Drs. Meyer Friedman and Ray H. Rosenmann as being highly competitive, excessively achievement-oriented, impatient, easily frustrated and angered, time-pressured and preoccupied with deadlines. Many perfectionists fit this description to a T.

Perfectionists are frequently lonely people. Since they are super-sensitive to criticism and always anticipating rejection or humiliation, they tend to withdraw from others. Since they overreact to even a hint of criticism, they often bring about the very disapproval and rejection they so much fear, and then crawl even deeper into their shells.

Not only do perfectionists set up unrealistic standards for themselves, but many of them expect superlative performances also from others. Because their expectations are constantly frustrated, they tend to be relentless critics of about everything and everybody. Also, since nothing even measures up to their standards, they miss out much that could be enjoyable.

Overgeneralizing

Another noteworthy characteristic of perfectionists is that they over-generalize. An isolated negative experience or failure is felt by them to portend similar failure-experiences in the future, no matter what they might attempt. They over-react to even relatively minor mistakes they make. Self-beratings such as "I'm always blundering," or "I'm no good, I'll never get this right," accompany many of their simple and correctable mistakes. In addition, they are plagued by what the renowned psychotherapist Karen Horney called "the tyranny of the shoulds". They always ought to have done this or that, mustn't make that blunder again, ought to have approached that problem differently, and so on.

Many perfectionists put off tasks that could take them closer to success because of their fear of failure. But procrastination only provides a temporary relief from worry and fear. In the long run it increases anticipatory anxiety and stress. Some procrastinators become completely immobilized. Their failure of effort is rationalized by an internal dialogue that says: "Since I can't do it perfectly, why bother at all?" And so they end up doing very little.

Peer Comparisons

Another source of misery for perfectionists is their habit of comparing their accomplishments to what their colleagues have achieved. Not only do they mistakenly perceive someone else's success as more successful than it frequently is, but they imagine that successful colleagues usually achieve their success with few if any mistakes, and little effort. This faulty perception of what successful attainment really entails further undermines their sense of adequacy. And they feel somehow cheated and defrauded by life.

Insight into these self-defeating attitudes and habits of thinking is sometimes sufficient to change some perfectionists into more realistic and less self-castigating persons. For others, however, therapeutic intervention is the only course to take.

Psychotherapy

One effective treatment for perfectionists is described by psychiatrist Dr. David D. Burns. He and his associates put their primary emphasis on changing the cognitive structure of the perfectionist.

As a first step in treating perfectionists, they urge them to make a list of the advantages of attempting to be perfect. As clients balance the costs against the benefits, they frequently become aware for the first time that perfectionism is not to their advantage. That awareness enhances their motivation to work towards giving it up. Until the perfectionist has arrived at that conclusion, it is fruitless to treat the disorder. Hari was able to list only one advantage of perfectionism: It can produce fine work. I'll try hard to come up with an excellent result. He listed six disadvantages: "One, it makes me so tense I can't work at times. Two, I am often unwilling to risk the mistakes necessary to come up with a creative piece of work. Three, my perfectionism inhibits me from trying new approaches and making discoveries because I am so preoccupied with being 'safe'. Thus, my world becomes narrow and I lose out on the opportunity for new challenges. Four, it makes me self-critical and takes the fun out of life. Five, I can't ever relax because I'll always find something that isn't perfect. Six, it makes me intolerant of others because I am constantly aware of the errors people make, and I end up being perceived as a fault-finder."

It did not take long for Hari to conclude that his life would be more rewarding and productive without perfectionism.

Maximizing Resources

Successful people know that perfection can never be attained and they recognize the limits of their talents and resources. But they all strive to become competent and do the best they can with whatever resources they have at hand. They don't have the time or inclination to worry about perfection or failure at each step along the way to a project's completion. And curiously enough, this freedom from anxiety and guilt over not attaining extra high standards helps many of them to come very close to perfection.

There are many gradations of excellence and success and just by aiming and persevering in doing things well, instead of perfectly, one can move into the comforting light of realistic self-perception of what one may actually achieve in one's chosen profession. (This exercise was devised by Princeton Creative Research, Inc., U.S.A.).

Epitaph Goal

Purpose : Determining and preparing to achieve your life's goals.

Posture : Immaterial.

Duration : Ten minutes at a time.

Procedure

Step-1

Imagine that today is the last day of your life. Write your own testament by completing the following sentences:

These are the things I have loved in life (things I tasted, looked at, smelt, heard, touched).

These experiences I have cherished.

These ideas I have profited from; and have had an impact on my life.

These beliefs I have outgrown.

These convictions I have lived by.

These things I have lived for.

These insights I have gained in the school of life (insight into God, the world, human nature, love, religion, life).

These risks I took, these dangers I have courted.

These sufferings have seasoned me.

These lessons life has taught me.

These influences have shaped my life (persons, occupations, books, events).

These religious texts have lit my path.

These things I regret about my life:

These are my life's achievements.

These are my life's unfulfilled desires.

(Step-1 was devised by Fr. Anthony de Mello. This testament gives an idea of your life's achievements so far. Ponder it for some time, adding to it if necessary until you have a pretty good assessment of yourself till now).

Step-2

Take a sheet of paper. Imagine it is your tombstone where a part of your ashes will be stored. Write your epitaph on it. What would you strongly desire to be remembered for, by posterity? For example: "Here lies XYZ who served his brethren and held their welfare above his own"; "Here lies XYZ who gave hope to the destitute"; "Here lies the woman who enhanced the lives of numerous of her sisters"; etc.

Step-3

Compare the conclusions from Steps 1 & 2. How much remains to be done to accomplish your life goals as expressed in your tombstone?

A) Outline the steps you need to take to accomplish this goal.

B) How much of this can you accomplish in two years (be specific)?

C) What specific steps (instrumental acts) do you plan to take to achieve that goal?

D) What blocks in yourself will you have to overcome to achieve that goal?
E) What blocks in the world will you have to overcome to achieve that goal?
F) How do you feel about the possibility of achieving that goal?
G) How do you feel about the possibility of failing to achieve it?
H) Where exactly will you go for help in accomplishing your goal?
I) How strongly do you want to achieve your goal?
J) How important is this goal as compared to other things you want out of life.

(List from "Motivating Economic Achievement" by David McClelland and David Winter).

The goal should be clear and specific. "To be more efficient", "Better family life", "More happiness", are too vague to be of any use. Even "to start a business" is not specific enough. It is preferable to set your (1) long term goal, (2) its purpose — viz, why you have set this goal, and (3) steps leading to the long-term goal.

For example : Your long-term goal could be: Setting up a beauty parlour

Purpose : a) Financial independence
b) To work for oneself

Short term goals : a) Do a course in cosmetology
b) Look out for a suitable location to set up the parlour
c) Work out the cost of such an enterprise
d) Where to obtain finance?
e) Publicity

To set these goals and purpose, do the following exercise:

Sit comfortably. Close your eyes. Relax all your muscles from head to foot. Count backwards from 100 to 1. If you lose count in between, start all over again anywhere in between and proceed till 1. When you feel very relaxed, let your mind wander in the direction of whatever changes you would like to carry out in your life. First select the area in which you want the changes: career, family life, health, hobbies, emotional well-being, etc.

When you have selected the most important area for change, get more specific. What new career? A holiday home for the family? Loss of weight? Collecting rare coins? Handling depression? When you have got that worked out, ask yourself what purpose you will achieve by attaining your goal. Finally, enumerate the steps you will have to take to achieve the goal. Imagine in detail going through all the necessary steps, achieving your goal and your ultimate purpose. Count from 1 to 3, saying to yourself that you will feel awake and alert at the count of 3. Then make a list of your short and long term goals and your purpose. Repeat this exercise at least three times in as many days, making alterations in the original plan if need be.

Step-4: Where to Get the Time or Energy

Relax as in step 3, counting from 100 to 1 and work out how much time and energy your activities leading to your goal will need. Do you have the time? Or will you have to cut into your present activities? If so which activities are you able and willing to discard and for how long?

Repeat the exercise over several sessions until you are satisfied that (1) you can do it; (2) that you really want to do it; (3) when you can do it. It is possible that you will find that the time and energy-cost of your goal is not worthwhile and that you would rather give up the goal. If so it is better to give it up now and look for a more achievable goal, rather than chase after something unattainable. In that case go back to step 2 select another goal, perhaps a preparatory step to your final goal.

Step-5: Result Imaging

Relax the usual way. Better still count backwards from 300 to 1 after scanning your body for tension and relaxing all your muscles. Then recall as vividly as you can successes you may have had with any projects in the past, so that a sense of pride and elation comes to you. (Whenever you feel in need of extra confidence, get into relaxation counting from 10 to 1, and recall these successes. You will feel a sense of fresh confidence). Then say to yourself: I shall succeed with my new goal as I did in my past project. Proceed to imagine in detail how your life will change on attaining your goal. This will help to keep your motivation to achieve your goal high. You will be mentally used to having achieved your goal and will not be able to do without it; it will become a need. You will also perceive yourself in a new light — as an achiever who can do what it takes to achieve results.

If you find it difficult to imagine yourself achieving your goal, picture someone else whom you admire achieving it. Then put yourself in his/her place. Enjoy in detail your achieved goal in every possible aspect, first watching yourself like a spectator, then merging the spectator into yourself as the actor. Do this exercise every day for ten to twenty minutes a day.

At the end of each exercise give yourself credit for achieving your goal.

Step-6: Process Imaging

Take out the list of items you need to achieve your goal. Go through the relaxation procedure and imagine the first item in the list, arranged in the order of priorities, from the simplest to the most difficult. Picture it in detail, how and when you are going to tackle this. If necessary, to give you ideas, get an imaginary friend to advise you on what to do to set this item done with. This adviser can be either mythological like Lord Krishna or historical like Nehru, or your boss, or someone you greatly respect. Enact an imaginary conversation with him/her and ideas will emerge. It will also make the problem solving more enjoyable. Do the exercise a couple of times a day till the first item has been tackled. If obstacles come up, consult your adviser, during your next exercise, on how to overcome it. After each item on your goal list is accomplished, congratulate yourself and proceed with the exercise, focusing on the next item on the list. Also keep doing the goal imagery exercise often, until the final goal is achieved.

Simultaneously review your achievement plan every three or six months with some close friend, or well-wisher.

Step-7

At the end of two years, review the extent of the success of the plan and draw up a plan for the next two years taking into account what you have learnt from your first 2-year plan, until your tombstone goal is achieved.

Achievement Boosters

Purpose : To aid in the efficient achievement of your goals.

Posture : Sitting.

Duration : Twenty minutes to half hour.

Procedure

Step-1

Sit comfortably where you won't be disturbed. Close your eyes. Relax all your muscles from head to foot consciously. Take three deep breaths. Count backwards form 100 to 1. If you lose count start again anywhere and proceed till you reach 1. Keep your eyes closed.

Step-2

Imagine you are in your sitting room in front of your TV set where you see a tele-serial with yourself as the main actor. Think of a goal you want to achieve, or a problem to resolve. Bring into the serial all the others involved in your goal or your problem. Act out your problem, or present situation, *not* the goal. Imagine yourself leaving the scene and sitting back in a chair in your sitting room. Freeze the scene on the TV set and stamp a big red NO on the screen.

Try to imagine all your feelings relating to the scene draining out of you, and try to imagine yourself free of these feelings. How do you feel?

Step-3

Pick someone you admire or respect, real or imaginary, who seems capable of solving your problem. Get him to act in the second instalment of the film serial. He will be playing your role. Visualise your chosen actor—Einstein, Shakespeare, Tagore, Shobha De, anyone—successfully achieving the goal you have in mind. Let all the other actors play their new roles in the changed situation with your goal accomplished. Let a voice tell you when this goal will be accomplished. "This will be realised by this date". Freeze the scene. Stamp the word 'Better' on it in bold golden colours.

Step-4

In the third instalment you re-enact the second instalment with yourself again as the main actor, replacing your earlier chosen actor, but achieving exactly the same goal in the same way. Watch yourself having achieved the goal. Freeze the scene and stamp it 'Better and Better'.

Step-5

Repeat the exercise thrice for each goal for three consecutive days. Perform steps 1 to 4 on first day; steps 1, 3 and 4 on second day; and only step 4 on final day.

This exercise, slightly modified, is taught by Silva Mind Control. Many former skeptics testify that it has worked for them.

2

Master Your Innovativeness

Sandip was the marketing manager at a multi-product company. He was doing well but not satisfied with his performance. He wanted to start new product lines. But when he suggested one such line, for air fresheners, he was asked to present a project report, but the management did not take it seriously, though it could find nothing wrong with the proposal. So Sandip advertised for a partner willing to invest in such a project. He found one, resigned from his job, formed a new partnership and successfully launched the project.

He now had another idea, for a water purifier, but his partner had his hands full and was unwilling to make further investments. So Sandip again advertised for a financier and launched his new project, just as successfully as the previous one. He now decided he had a knack for innovation and set himself up as a consultant, advising companies on diversification of their product lines. His strategy consisted of an amalgam of approaches based on ideas drawn from Peter Drucker, Edward de Bono and other management thinkers. They are described in detail below:

Where to Look for Innovative Opportunities

Purpose : To search for needs that innovation can fulfil.

Duration : Ten-minute segments.

Posture : Immaterial.

Procedure

Peter Drucker defined innovation as a social or economic term rather than as a technical term. "It can be defined", he said, "the way J.B. Say defined entrepreneurship, as changing the yield or resources. Or, as a modern economist would tend to do, it can be defined in demand terms rather than in supply terms, that is, as changing the value and satisfaction obtained from resources by the consumer".

McDonald's fast food chain innovated by mass producing what was already being produced in individual restaurants, by creating "a new market and a new customer". Cyrus McCormick, a harvesting machine inventor, created an innovation when he conceived of instalment buying which enabled farmers to buy their machines from their future earnings, and thus opened a huge new market of investment buyers who previously could not afford to buy these or other goods that came under its preview. The important thing about innovation is that it is demand-driven, in Drucker's term. That is, demand gives it value. Innovators "try to create new and different values and new and different satisfactions, to convert a 'material' into a 'resource', or to combine existing resources into a new and more productive configuration".

Drucker has pinpointed seven sources of innovative opportunity that should be encompassed in any systematic search for innovative opportunities:

1) *The unexpected*

a) Success

b) Failure or

c) Outside event.

a) **Unexpected Success:** When confronted with an unexpected success in their product lines, managements should immediately consider how they can fully exploit it, where it would lead the company and how it can be converted into an opportunity. When Japanese farmers began to buy colour TV sets in great numbers, contrary to all expectations, Matsushita, owner of National and Panasonic, sold them door-to-door, a first time practice in Japan for any consumer durable, to exploit the demand, and rose to the top. The first computers were designed for scientific research. But when IBM discovered that they were being bought by companies for calculating salaries, it immediately attained leadership among computer manufactureres by designing computers for business.

b) **Unexpected Failure:** When a meticulously laid out plan fails for no apparent reason, an opportunity awaits. In the 1920s a British manufacturer of padlocks in India found his sales in the country dwindling. He improved the design making it safer, but the product failed completely in finding buyers and he went into liquidation. A competitor, however, found out the padlock had two traditional markets, one in the village, the other in the city. The city market needed a safer lock, which it got when the manufacturer redesigned its old padlock. But the city market was small. The larger farmer's market consisted of people for whom the lock was only a symbol of safety, and they tended to lose the keys. When they lost the keys the improved locks became a nuisance since they were more difficult to open. The old ones at least could be easily opened. So they stopped buying them. What the original manufacturer's competitor did was build two locks: 1) a safe one for the city, at a high price and high profit margin; and 2) a lock without a key, only with a release mechanism, but much cheaper than the original padlock and with twice its profit margin. Both sold well in their respective markets and the firm held a leadership position for over a decade.

c) **Unexpected Outside Event:** Retail stores in America successfully took up the sale of books which were previously stored only by bookshops, when they realised that Americans buy books but don't collect them after reading. That is, a book is like any other consumer item, to be discarded after use. So Americans would like to find books where they could find any other consumer item, and buy them on impulse.

2) ***Incongruities:*** That is, "a dissonance between what is and what 'ought' to be, or between what is and what everybody assumes it to be."

These can be:

a) **Economic Incongruities:** For example, there is great demand for health care, but the cost is still very high. To provide inexpensive health care, profitably, is an opportunity that has not yet been fully exploited;

b) **Incongruity between Reality and Assumptions about It:** Arrival of airfreight appeared to spell the end of ocean-freight which was increasing in cost. The innovation in containerisation, loading in standard sized metal containers which enabled the loading to be done on land, at no cost to ships' waiting time at anchorage, led to five-fold increase in ocean freight traffic in thirty years, and a lowering of costs.

c) **Incongruity between Perceived and Actual Customer Values and Expectations:** Share brokers operate on the assumption that people invest to become rich and devote all their time to investment. Mutual funds were successful because they understood most people invest to maximise their savings, and have no time for speculative investment. By managing their clients' money they exploit that need.

It is important to understand what exactly a customer is buying. He himself may not know what value he gets out of a product. When a product is supplied which is not 'valued' by the customer, and thus is a failure in the market, it is probably because the customer is looking for some other 'value' in the product, which is not being provided. It would be worthwhile to find out what the customer is looking for, seek a congruity between the actual values and expectations of the customer and what you are providing.

d) **Incongruity in the Internal Logic of a Process:** During the 1950s William Connor, a pharmaceutical company salesman, discovered that in the simple and routine cataract operating procedure, one stage was potentially risky: cutting the ligament and tying the blood vessels, could risk bleeding and endangering the eye. Connor found that an enzyme existed which could dissolve the ligament, but no one had found a way to preserve the enzyme.

Through some simple trial and error research he found such a preservative; patented it, and marketed the enzyme, which every eye surgeon began to use.

It should be easy to detect such a lacuna between need and availability, that delays or complicates an otherwise smooth process. But it is usually discernable only to those already familiar with the process, not to outsiders.

3) Process Need: Early in the century Bell Telephones plotted two graphs: one was of the US population growth; the other of the number of women needed to operate telephone switchboards. The graphs showed that all the available women would not be sufficient to operate the number of manual switchboards that would be operating by 1930. So it designed and built the first automatic switchboard.

There was great demand for cameras among amateur photographers long before the end of the last century, but the glass plate technology was cumbersome and unsuitable, and the cameras were uncomfortably heavy. George Eastman of Kodak replaced the glass plate with film, which also made possible the use of light cameras. Within a decade Eastman Kodak soared to leadership position in cameras.

As Drucker points out "successful innovations based on process needs require five basic criteria: a self-contained process; one 'weak' or 'missing' link; a clear definition of objective; that the specifications for the solution be defined clearly; widespread realisation that 'there ought to be a better way', that is, high receptivity".

However, the process needs to be well understood, technology must be available to do the job, and the innovation must be suited to the way people operate or want to operate.

4) Industry and Market Structures: How should industry respond to market needs? The automobile industry reacted in different ways: Rolls-Royce supplied the royalty imprint; Ford produced the first mass consumption car; Fiat supplied the military staff car. Germany produced the VW Beetle people car. Later, the Japanese broke into the US market with their fuel efficient cars. Each met a need based on changing industrial and social structures, successfully.

The growth of health care in hospitals in the U.S. of the 1960s led one innovator to supply housekeeping services like kitchen, laundry, maintenance to hospitals.

The indicators of change in industrial structures are:

a) rapid growth outstripping economic or population growth;
b) existing market unable to keep up with industry growth;
c) confluence of technologies in one application as that of telephone and computer technologies in electronic private branch exchange (EPABX) switchboards;
d) rapid change in business' modus operandi.

Innovations in this area are particularly effective if the industry is dominated by very few large manufacturers, or a single one. For example the monopoly of the postal department was successfully broken by umpteen courier services who could provide quick, reliable, delivery of parcels. Simplicity of operation, however, is essential for success in this area.

5) Population Changes: Like baby booms, rising income levels, literacy rates, change in labour force, etc. These may be unpredictable, "yet they do have long lead times before impact, and lead times, moreover that are predictable", says Drucker. Important indicators are age distribution; sex ratio; change in lifestyle.

6) Change in Perception: How do people see themselves? Are they status conscious? Health conscious? Do women see themselves as equal to men? Environment conscious? What are the symbols of their new perceptions? TV, cars, jeans, jogging, natural food? Timing is crucial in exploiting the new perceptions. One has to be first to rake in the most.

7) New Technologies: Innovation based on emerging knowledge requires:

a) careful analysis of a wide variety of factors—economic, social, psychological—that will be instrumental in the successful application of the new knowledge;

b) a clear thought-out strategy involving (i) a complete self-sustaining system; (ii) a market focus; (iii) key functions;

c) entrepreneurial management.

One of the riskiest sources of innovation is the bright idea, taken in isolation.

Principles of Innovation: Do's and Don'ts

Do's

1) Begin with the analysis of the opportunities.
2) "Innovation is both conceptual and perceptual".

So, look, ask, listen. Look at figures as well as at people. Use both sides of your brain, analytical and intuitive.

3) Be simple and focused.
4) Start small; try to do one specific thing.
5) Aim at leadership, not necessarily the biggest, but try to be the king of your niche.

Don'ts

1) Don't try to be cleverer than you can help.
2) Don't diversify; concentrate.
3) Don't innovate for the future but for now, taking note of conditions prevailing now.

Conditions for Successful Innovation

1) Innovation involves sustained purposeful work.
2) Build on your strengths, knowledge, capabilities. Make sure you fit in, in every respect, that you have command over every aspect of your innovation.
3) Innovation has a social and economic impact. It has to be 'market-driven'.

Programme Your Mind for Innovation

Purpose : To remove perceptual and conceptual blocks to creativity and programme your mind to perceive and develop ideas into innovations.

Duration : Unlimited, in ten-minute segments.

Posture : Immaterial.

Procedure

1) ***Be Aware of Your Blocks to Creative Thinking and Try to Eliminate Them***

   a) **Perceptual Blocks:** Way of handling information, inability to see a problem, preconceived ideas, inability to work on a problem on a broad scale, putting unnecessary restrictions on it, not being able to see a problem from another person's point of view, failure to use all your sense organs in solving a problem.

   b) **Emotional Blocks:** Fear of ridicule; fear of failure; tendency to be overjudgemental to new ideas; need to get job done fast; inability to relax; inability to allow one's fantasy life and day-dreams to run wild; lack of motivation.

   c) **Cultural Blocks:** The view that intuition and theories are bad, fear of change, belief that you need money to be creative.

   d) **Environmental Blocks:** That is factors in the environment that prevent creativity: ridicule, indifference, lack of available time, lack of organisational and financial support, distractions that interfere with production of ideas.

   e) **Intellectual Blocks:** Choosing wrong techniques or thinking mode, inability to separate correct from incorrect information. Imprecise nature of our language and expression.

2) ***Breaking the Blocks***

   a) Creative thinking should be done when your body temperature is at its peak—take your temperature every hour.

   b) Before achieving something you must be able to

conceive it. Visualise yourself, under relaxed conditions, coming up with creative ideas. Feel confident and proud of being creative. Do this every day at a particular time.

c) Think of some problem you have and write it down as concisely as possible. State the problem in different ways and try to find a solution to each statement. Redefine the problem from a different point of view. Some in very broad terms; some in very narrow terms. Next time you have a problem, solve it your normal way, then write the problem from a different point of view and try to find a different solution.

d) Pick a problem you have with another person. Write a statement of the problem as you see it. Write it down as the other person would see it. Then write it down as a third person would see it. Try to find a solution acceptable to yourself and the one with whom you have the problem. Check with him/her.

e) Become aware of what you think of people and why. Is it because of their height, voice, social status, position, dress, confidence?

f) If you are afraid of looking foolish do things purposely that will make you look foolish to bring your fear under control.

g) Write down what would happen if your ideas were completely wrong. The world will not end.

h) Try to solve each problem: i) visually; ii) verbally, that is, with words; iii) mathematically.

i) Add 'what if' to your vocabulary. Never be satisfied with the way things are. Develop your own problem list. Write down everything that bothers you about everything. Write non-stop, for at least 15 minutes and come up with at least 100 items from 'clock not working' to 'famine in India'. Go around asking questions, listen to the answers, to people's opinions.

j) One way of getting ideas is to make lists. Don't be judgemental in the beginning. If you are working with others exchange lists. You will crossfertilise your ideas.

k) Brainstorm, suspend judgement and produce as many ideas as you can. Then modify your ideas through i) five-sensing, that is think of the effect of your ideas on the modalities of sight, sound, touch, taste, smell; ii) putting the ideas to other uses; iii) adapting; iv) modifying; v) magnifying vi) substituting; vii) combining; viii) reversing its components; ix) subtracting portions; x) minimising; xi) rearranging.

l) Do a manipulative checklist: multiply, divide, eliminate, subdue, invert, separate, transpose, unify, distort, flatten, squeeze, complement, submerge, freeze, fasten, slip-up, bypass, add, subtract, lighten, repeat, stretch, extend, repel, protect, segregate, integrate, symbolise, abstract, dissect, etc.

m) Practise visualising your spouse, friends, etc, then check with the reality. Then change their features. Do this playfully, as absurdly as you can. Practise all your sense modalities.

n) Have a personalised creative space in your mind, conducive to relaxation, so that you can close you eyes and live comfortably in that environment when you want to do some thinking.

3) Creative Control System: Sit comfortably. Close your eyes, take three deep breaths. Progressively relax all your muscles from head to foot. When you feel pleasantly relaxed, tell yourself: "Tomorrow morning I will get the ideas that I need". If you are working on a specific problem, review all the facts relating to it, then tell yourself "Tomorrow after waking up the answers will come to me". The control system works best when practised before going to sleep at night.

3

Master Thinker's Toolbox

This is a survey of Edward de Bono's lateral thinking techniques and an assessment of their effectiveness.

Purpose : To augment your repertoire of creative tools.

Posture : Immaterial.

Duration : Can be practised in ten-minute segments, if necessary, but the longer you use them the more adept you are likely to be in achieving the results you seek.

"The information age is already gone. The emphasis is on thinking and ideas. Our problem is what to do with the information available." That is Edward de Bono speaking. One has come to expect provocative statements from him. It is the easiest way to draw the attention of corporations and get them to invite him to conduct seminars for them. De Bono has conducted seminars for the world's leading companies, like IBM, 3M, Prudential Insurance, Du Pont and even the Tatas. Provocation is also an important device in de Bono's toolbox of concepts to make thinking more effective.

De Bono is best known as the father of lateral thinking, a term which, as he never tires of reminding us, has found its way into the Oxford Dictionary. Lateral thinking, de Bono has boasted, is the greatest advance in thinking since Aristotle: one of his books' title is 'Parallel Thinking: From Socratic To De Bono Thinking.' He has also claimed that 3M R&D executives have acknowledged that his short talk on lateral thinking produced more results than years of research by the company. He has quoted Peter Ueberoth, responsible for the enormous commercial success of the Los Angeles Olympics, to the effect that the success was due entirely to the ideas he learned from de Bono in a seminar he had conducted. De Bono has also divulged that the Managing Director of the Japanese giant corporation Nippon Telephones and Telegraphs, after reading his book Six Thinking Hats, ordered 200 copies for his executives and following the prescription therein turned Nippon from a loss making enterprise into a highly profitable venture.

These are not all of his achievements. He has produced a stream of books, among them Mechanism of Mind where he propounds the theory that the brain is a self-organising system, supposedly a prescient notion now accepted by computer experts. He has also designed thinking courses for children which have been adopted in numerous countries. He maintains that intelligent people are not necessarily effective thinkers. They are adept at analysing data available to them, but are not used to changing their perceptions, which is the basis of lateral thinking, a much more fundamental activity than analytical thinking, in de Bono's view. He has even conducted The de Bono Thinking Course for the BBC, which has since been published in book form.

What exactly is lateral thinking and how does it work? According to the Oxford Dictionary, it is an unusual or apparently illogical way to solve a problem. It consists in using conceptual devices, which will be discussed below, as levers to help you vault out of conventional thinking patterns so you can perceive a situation in a new light. As de Bono himself puts it, "Lateral thinking has specifically to do with generating new ideas and perceptions. The computer may be able to work on the information available but only the human brain can go beyond and act on perception." He has said that 90% of thinking takes place at the perceptual stage and with the tremendous strides in analytical thinking and data processing, the need of effective thinking at the perceptual level becomes all the more apparent. It is perception that widens our vision and changes the scenario on which it acts.

To aid his readers and clients in lateral thinking de Bono has, in his several books, generated a cluster of concepts designed to jog the mind into "serious creativity" and enable it to perceive things differently. Here are some of these concepts:

1) PO or Provocative Operation: This concept, explained at length in PO: Beyond Yes and No, consists in trying for alternative ways of doing things, even if they seem absurd at first sight. For example, PO: "cars should have square wheels". The provocation should be followed by 'movement' of thought, that is, thinking where and how the provocation, seemingly absurd, could become practical. Square wheels could function if the terrain were so irregular that it would not matter whether they were square or round. This idea could result in a suspension for the car that would enable it to run over rugged terrain without discomfort for the passengers.

2) Plus, Minus, Interesting (PMI): This consists in examining each new idea for positive, negative and interesting but unclear aspects. This results in broadening our minds to seize new opportunities instead of falling prey to our prejudices. De Bono maintains that in his experience those who act after a PMI exercise often take decisions quite at variance with decisions they would normally have taken without its aid. If you were planning to buy a car, for example, you could find it more convenient, all aspects of the situation considered, to travel by taxi or hired car and invest the price of the car elsewhere.

3) Six Thinking Hats: This concept involves taking six different approaches to a problem, consecutively. Each approach is represented by a colour: white is for merely considering the bare data on it; green for unusual, offbeat ideas to solve it without judging the merit of the ideas at this stage; black for logical impediments to the solution; red for hunches, feelings and intuition; yellow for logically positive arguments; blue is the control colour that examines the thinking itself rather than the subject. You wear one hat at a time and operate according to the framework dictated by it while solving your problem. Using the Six Thinking Hats framework systematically in problem-solving should have the effect of broadening and balancing one's personality as well. If you are naturally analytical, wearing the red hat should force you to become intuitive as well. If you are a pessimist, the green hat will enable you to adopt the optimistic stance as well, making your perspective well rounded.

4) The Edge Effect: This consists in distinguishing the fundamental from the peripheral in a situation. If your purpose in buying a house is status, then location could become fundamental and comfort peripheral.

5) Idea Sensitive Area (ISA): It is the place where one believes new ideas will have a significant impact in changing the situation. Adding a new feature to your computer may be more important to get demand for it from customers than reducing the price, adding to its speed or even making it portable.

6) Considering All Factors (CAF): This consists in doing a systematic checklist to ensure that nothing relevant is missed. Buying an otherwise ideal business premise in a locality suffering from frequent power cuts could be a disastrous decision.

7) Consequences and Sequel (C&S): It helps select the best option, after you have generated various alternatives through PMI and CAF, by trying to imagine the probable outcome of each alternative. What would happen if the use of paper were banned? Considering the possibility could lead you to invent a better alternative even if paper were still in use.

8) Aims, Goals, Objectives: This consists in sorting out your reasons for taking any particular action. We don't always have clear goals and often end up with something we hadn't bargained for. This concept is intended to clarify our goals by uncovering hidden priorities. If your goal is to retire away from the city din, it would be a mistake to buy a house in a neighbourhood where everyone loves to play their music systems at maximum volume.

9) Other Point of View (OPV): In conflict situations, it is important to appreciate the opponent's point of view by stepping into his shoes and thinking as he would. In non-conflict situations, too, it is useful to take the view of a disinterested bystander or a prospective opponent. Reversing the situation in item 8, you may enjoy listening to loud music but you should consider your neighbours, too, before raising your system's volume to a level that may prove dangerous for your relations with them.

10) Water Logic: This is one of de Bono's terms which he uses to distinguish his own logic from traditional logic which he terms "rock logic" since it analyses only the structure of a situation, not its purpose. To illustrate: when de Bono's book Six Thinking Hats appeared, a critic commented that it had some good ideas in it but that they could easily have been explained in a short article and did not justify a full book. In other words the logic was: "Don't explain in 100,000 words when 1,000 will do." That is rock logic. But as I pointed out elsewhere, "though the charge is true, it misses two points. The first point is that for its author the book format is obviously the more profitable option. The other point is that a book, specially a bestseller, remains in the public eye for an incomparably longer time than an article and consequently has a longer life. De Bono's books have all been steady sellers worldwide for a long time and continue to be reprinted." Undoubtedly de Bono was using water logic when he wrote this book. In his book, Water Logic de Bono shows how a flow diagram of your thinking can be used to make your perceptions 'visible'. Says de Bono: "We can then try to intervene and see how our perceptions might be altered. Although we are intervening in the inner world of perception we can get suggestions that may also be useful for intervening in the outer world."

11) Parallel Thinking: "The first stage of parallel thinking is to do with laying down a field of parallel possibilities. Parallel thinking is concerned with 'possibilities' more than with judgement of 'truth'. What are you going to do with a possibility? You move forward to see what it contributes...With possibilities it is almost essential to use water logic. 'What happens next'."

12) Lateral Wisdom: It had to come, sooner or later, de Bono's own version of what is wisdom: "You choose the road you want according to your needs and values. The purpose of wisdom is to allow you to apply your values effectively. It is possible that over time, wisdom may get you to alter your values. The purpose of wisdom is to lay out the inner world and outer world in such a way that you can make choices." In other words, wisdom is how your perception moulds your experience to fit your values. De Bono tells you to listen to the whispers of perception rather than merely to the louder promptings of reason or logic. A bigger problem however arises when you listen neither to the voice of reason nor to the intimations of perception but to the call of emotion. Worse still, what do you do when your values are themselves flawed as in the case of Hitler, Marquis de Sade, Pol Pot and Stalin? De Bono has no convincing answer to that one.

The reader should be cautioned, however, that the wealth of ideas de Bono has generated does not guarantee their effectiveness in practice. Unless an idea is tested, one cannot be sure that it works although one may feel intuitively that it should. The scientific way to test such an idea is to get a group of people to use the idea to solve a problem and compare the result with the results of a control group of the same mental level using traditional techniques to solve the same problem. To the best of my knowledge no such research has been done. If it had, one can be sure de Bono would have been the first to cite the results if they favoured him. Another way to test his ideas would be to apply them in practice and determine for yourself how effective they are vis-a-vis your previous attempts at solving problems or handling a situation. In these days of TQM and Kaizen or continuous improvement, de Bono's ideas present themselves as ideal experimental tools awaiting to be tested. It is surprising however that de Bono, who never ceases to cite examples of how his ideas have influenced others, has given very few concrete examples of exactly how his ideas were applied and what specific outcomes they generated. Here are two such examples: "By using Edward de Bono's brilliant concept of 'lateral thinking' we were able to revolutionise the insurance industry through 'living needs' policies that allow people to benefit from their life insurance while they are still alive," writes Ron Barbaro, President, Prudential Insurance; "At Du Pont...lateral thinking led to a major breakthrough in process continuity at a fibre plant with a radical altering of basic equipment design, reducing the number of moving parts by 80%," writes David Tanner, Founding Director, Du Pont Centre of Creativity & Innovation. Neither Ueberoth nor the 3M researchers nor the Nippon chief get down to specifics. It is difficult to believe that de Bono would not have used more of these instances, were they available, to further publicise his ideas and books. Most of the examples in his books are hypothetical.

Another aspect of de Bono worth considering is how he himself generates his ideas. Readers conversant with writers on creativity and with de Bono's own work will have by now discovered that he is less original than he seems at first. For example, his favourite unconfessed tool for generating ideas has been analogy, a device originally propagated by William J. Gordon in his Synectics system. Gordon recommends four types of analogies (personal, direct, symbolic and fantasy-based) for greater creativity. Several of de Bono's books are based on a single analogy: Masterthinker's Handbook—A Guide for Innovative Thinking uses the analogy of the human body, calling it the Body Framework Theory (BFT). Similarly, his Handbook for a Positive Revolution uses the analogy of the hand and its five fingers to present its ideas. So, if you have ambitions to become a management writer, think of an analogy, a tree for example, and hang your ideas on it. Thus your book on quality could be titled The Tree of Quality and the various aspects of quality could be laid out in chapters titled The Roots of Quality, The Stem of Quality, The Branches of Quality, The Leaves of Quality, The Sap of Quality and finally The Fruits of Quality. That's how management writers are made!

4

Problem Solving: The 20-Question Method

Purpose : To find a solution to your problem through a systematic search.
Posture : Immaterial.
Duration : As long as it takes to answer the twenty questions.

Procedure

This technique has been suggested by Rudolf Flesch and is based on the 20-questions game in which the player tries to guess the answer to the question "What is it I have thought of?" by asking the person challenging him 20 non-leading questions, that is questions whose answers are 'Yes' or 'No'. In other words the question should take the form "Is it a —?".

The game begins with the challenger stating whether the object he has thought of is from the animal, vegetable or mineral kingdom.

Here is a sample of the game as played on radio, given by Flesch himself, but slightly modified for simplicity sake.

Challenger : It's a vegetable.

Q(1) Player : It is wood or a wood product?

Challenger : Yes.

Q(2) P : Is it wood?

C : It's wood.

Q(3) P : Does this thing exist ?

C : No.

Q(4) P : If it did exist would it be manufactured?

C : Yes, if it did exist it would be manufactured.

Q(5) P : Is it connected with one professional person?

C : Yes it is.

Q(6) P : Was it large enough to carry people in it?

C : No: What were you thinking of?

P : The Trojan Horse.

C : No, It isn't.

Q(7) P : Is this in American fiction?

C : No.

Q(8) P : Is it in British fiction?

C : Yes, it's partly there.

Q(9) P : Is it in prose fiction?

C : Yes, it is in that form, too.

Q(10) P : Is it small enough to be carried about?

C : No.

Q(11) P : Is it a building?

C : No, not a building.

Q(12) P : Is it a means of transportation?

C : No, it is not.

Q(13) **P** : When it's manufactured, is it put together with something else?
C : Yes, usually.

Q(14) **P** : With things like nails, etc?
C : Yes, usually that's how it is done.

Q(15) **P** : Is it a piece of furniture?
C : Yes.

Q(16) **P** : Is it a chair?
C : No.

Q(17) **P** : A round table?
C : Yes, it is.

Q(18) **P** : King Arthur's Round Table?
C : Yes, you've guessed it!

Flesch advises players of this game not to waste questions with wild guesses, ask questions that have "an even chance" of being right, and to vary their approach. Ask a question that would eliminate or confirm a large class of possibilities, e. g. : "Is it wood or wood product?"

In your own 20-questions game there is no challenger to answer your questions. You have to ask and answer them yourself. If you don't know the answer you can put it down as 'probably yes' or 'probably no'. If you don't know that either it may be possible to find out. And of course there is no need to stick to just 20 questions—ask as many as you need to get your answer!

Flesch also suggests that new or unusual classifications may provide a solution to your problem.

For example, you can classify games as competitive, noncompetitive, indoor, outdoor, involving hands, feet, or both, ball games, card games, needing racquets, (golf)clubs, (hockey)sticks, duration wise etc. Possibly through such a classification one-day cricket was invented."New classifications will often completely change our attitudes and our thinking," says Flesch. He sums up his own recommendations for creative problem solving as follows:

1) Try to remember that everyone including yourself has only his own experience to think of. Try exchanging ideas with other people. Conversation is a great generator of ideas.
2) Try to detach your ideas from your words.
3) Translate the abstract and general into the specific and concrete.
4) To solve a puzzling problem look for a seemingly irrelevant key factor in the situation and for a seemingly unsuitable pattern in your mind.
5) Narrow the field of solutions by asking 'twenty questions'.
6) Remember that bright ideas are often wrong and must be tested.
7) Don't underrate the influence of chance.

To these he adds the following list of tips:

1) Write the problem down.
2) Translate the problem into plain English.
3) If possible translate the problem into figures, mathematical symbols, or graphs.
4) Don't rely on your memory for facts, but check them out.
5) Learn to use a library.
6) Take notes and keep files.
7) Use a check list of categories, adding new ones from time to time.

8) Try turning the problem upside down.
9) Don't be afraid of the ridiculous.
10) If you feel frustrated, don't worry. Relax, turn to other work, rest, sleep.
11) Take time to be by yourself. Free yourself from trivial work. Shut out interruptions.
12) Know the time of day when your mind works best and arrange your schedule accordingly.
13) When you get an idea write it down.

5

LEAP INTO THE CREATIVE REALM

Purpose : To learn yet another approach to create the things you desire.
Posture : Immaterial.
Duration : Can be practised in 10-minute segments, if necessary.

"Creating is a skill that can be learned and mastered. People from all walks of life, and from all backgrounds, can learn to create, in the same way that they can learn to drive a car, swim or use a computer." That's Robert Fritz speaking. He is the founder of DMA, Inc., and developer of the Technologies For Creating curriculum. In the last two decades his DMA seminars have trained some 50,000 people in the creative process in more than 24 countries. His trainees have included Fortune 500 executives as also leaders in the fields of science, technology, arts and entertainment. He goes on to say: "As a skill, creating can be used in many realms. When used in music or painting, the results are artistic, When used in technology, the results are invention. When used in business, the results are production... When creating is used to build your life, the results are often tremendous involvement, vitality, adventure and expansion. I have discovered many principles that can help you learn and develop your creative process—principles that can encompass the many facets of your life. Through working with these, you will begin to see how your life itself can be the subject of the creative process."

What are these principles which Fritz has discovered and successfully used as a writer, painter, composer and entrepreneur? Here they are:

1. The Driving Force: You need a constant supply of energy to pursue your creative goal to fruition. You won't get it unless you are clear about what your goal is. Are you after a specific result which you would love to see created for its own sake, or are you merely trying to change an existing condition? It's important to know the difference. Whether you wish to develop a training programme, compose a song, or design some computer software, your goal should not be merely a reaction to an existing condition, or mitigate a current dissatisfaction, but to create a new outcome or product.

2. *Creating versus Creativity:* People tend to confuse the creative process with producing something unusual, generally associated with creativity. Often that's what is produced, but not always. You can create what you want without summoning creativity to your aid. Likewise creativity can produce unusual ideas but nothing more tangible. 'Unusual' or 'inventive' are not the issue when creating; are you producing what you want to? That's the question.

3. Form versus Formula: Fritz stresses that there is no formula for creating, but that it does have a form, consisting of a series of steps. If you reduce your creation to a formula, you are working against yourself. Knowing the steps to be taken to get to your goal by your own route will help you get there efficiently.

4. Results versus Process: Many putative creators get bogged down in the process of creating before knowing what they want to create. Fritz emphasises that you cannot think of how to get somewhere before knowing where that 'somewhere' is. So concentrate on the results you want to achieve before you consider how to achieve them.

5. The Unknown and the Known: Make sure you know the difference between observation and speculation and don't confuse the two. When you are dealing with the unknown, any thoughts about it are speculation. Since creating involves producing something new, it's still unknown until you have created it. But you can only start with the existing or the known, that is, from current reality which can be accessed only through observation, not speculation. Speculation can never lead to creation unless it based on solid observation.

6. The Knowable and the Unknowable: You must also distinguish between what can be known, whether or not you happen to know it now, and what you cannot possibly know. It is tempting to fill the gaps of knowledge with speculation which is destructive of your goal. The unknown has to be first divided into the knowable and the unknowable, and then the knowable but as yet unknown can be made known through observation and investigation, keeping away from the illusion of knowing the unknowable through speculation.

7. Instinctive and Self-conceived Tension-Resolution Systems: Your creation will be the result of your vision of what you want to bring about. The gap between your vision and the current reality with respect to what you want to create, results in what Fritz calls 'structural tension' which gets resolved when your vision becomes reality. There is sometimes a temptation to reduce the tension in the shortest possible time by settling for a goal that will not be to your liking or of a quality below what you may have been able to otherwise achieve. It is advisable to postpone the resolution of the tension strategically until you craft a goal of the standard and quality you are capable and proud of achieving.

8. Learners and Performers: Performers believe that they have reached the height of their capabilities and try to perform always to the best of their assumed abilities. The learners, on the other hand, believe they can learn newer, better ways of what they have been doing, even if they suffer temporary setbacks on their way to learning new skills. The learning approach is the more fruitful in generating quality results.

9. Choice and Obligation: What you create and how is a matter of your choice. You can evade responsibility by believing that you are fulfilling an obligation, but in doing so you may opt for second best actions towards your goal which you attribute to your obligation. The only obligation you have is to exercise your choices honestly.

10. Stretch and Consolidate: When you explore the new, the unusual or the unfamiliar, you stretch your capabilities, until through repetition these areas become familiar and routine. The process helps you acquire, consolidate and master previously non-existent skills.

11. Separation and Oneness: Your creation is not a part of you. It is important that you realise it so you can bring to it an essential sense of detachment from it which would be missing if you felt a sense of oneness with it. Separateness is necessary to establish the appropriate relationship between you and your creation.

12. First-person/Third-person Orientation: Certain prospective creators are excessively self-preoccupied. This first person orientation unduly limits the possibilities of what they create. A third person orientation directed at the object of creation, rather than themselves is more efficient and productive in the creative process.

13. Ideals versus Reality: People have all sorts of ideals and beliefs about themselves which limit their achievements. Fritz believes that how good or bad you feel about yourself is irrelevant to the creative process. Concentrating on your creation and the steps to achieve it, rather than on the creator himself, will help you avoid the pitfalls associated with low self-esteem.

14. Worldview versus Creating: Don't let your ideas of how the universe runs interfere with what you are creating. These ideas are either true or false and nothing you think can change the reality. But they can interfere, if you let them, with the quality of your creation.

15. Absolute and Relative Truth: Leave the question what is the nature of truth and such things outside the purview of your creation. Stick to what is achievable which is in the realm of relative truth.

16. Burden or Blessing: When you consider the burdens of life you are thinking of your dissatisfaction with the current situation. When you are engaged in the creative process you are using life's blessings which enables you to exercise choices in life.

17. Creating Your Life—Creating Individual Creations in Your Life: Your life is made up of innumerable small things. You cannot build up your life as a whole, but you can create the things you love and they will contribute the quality of your life as a whole.

18. Active—Passive: The rhythm of creation consists of alternating active and passive periods. Settle into your own creative personal rhythm best suited to you and the object of your creation.

To sum up then let us consider the creative process as envisioned by Fritz using the foregoing benchmarks. First comes the stage of conception of the result you want. Do not confuse your creation with problem solving which is designed to get rid of a current dissatisfaction, nor should you confuse it with a step in the process towards achieving your goal, for example, going on a diet, studying yoga, etc. which are not ends in themselves. "It is easy to determine the assumed end result from a process step if you ask the question, what is the step designed to do, or once I have accomplished this step, what result will I have?," Fritz advises. "In the conceptual stage you are experimenting with ideas. You have not yet formed the final end result you want. Instead you are trying many end results to see how they play. The experience you gain by gradually forming your ideas helps you learn more about the end result you finally want to create."

The second step is vision. Here you zero in on a specific end result. You may not have worked out all the details yet, but you know the overall form. For example, you may want to write a book on management. You may not yet have decided whether it is going to be a comparative study of prominent ideas on quality, or a book of case studies on how quality has been promoted, or a book on an entirely new paradigm about quality. "Some people", says Fritz, "think they must decide on an end result all at once and consequently settle on a first impression. First impressions are usually not well-considered. Even if you have a wonderful first impression of an end result, if it is truly wonderful you will still have it after you have played with it." It is advisable to let your goal rest on the shelf for a while before deciding it is exactly what you want.

The next step is an assessment of current reality. Fritz is of the view that creators find much greater difficulty in assessing current reality relevant to their goals than discovering what exactly they want to create. Yet its importance cannot be overemphasised. Even in a simple matter like organising a meeting, you have to consider current facilities. What do you need for the meeting? A room, ten chairs, note pads, projection equipment, facilities for tea. Do you have them all? If not your meeting can end in disaster. So much more in case of more complex creations. A realistic assessment of current reality and the gap between it and your vision will create the tension that will be resolved only when your creation takes final shape.

The fourth step is to take action. "Although many people may know much about the steps that will help them move from where they are to where they want to go, still they wait, and wait and wait. Why? Because there are no guarantees that their actions will work..." says Fritz. "It is important to balance planning with action. Plans lead to actions that produce direct experience of the plans. This leads to correcting their plans..." and further action and better knowledge of what it takes to achieve your final result.

The fifth step is to "adjust—learn—evaluate—adjust." This is a learning process that is not only intellectual but visceral as you internalise the process through practice.

The sixth step is building momentum. This can be done by using deadlines to organise your actions. Going backwards from your deadline for the final result, you establish a deadline for each previous step.

The seventh step is to "always have a place to go". That is keep the next step always in mind and be ready for action on it.

The eighth step is completion. You have achieved your result. You compare it with what you had in mind, make some adjustments, again compare and still make some more changes, until you decide that this is it. Some people, says Fritz, never complete a project. It may be useful to have another project in mind to enable you to fight this tendency.

The last step is living with your creation. You may not be immediately satisfied with your creation. Your attitude to it may change over time. You may like it better or worse. If worse you may use it to learn to improve on your next creation.

6

MASTER YOUR INTUITION

Abdul was a successful lawyer. He was married to Shernaz, a beautician and a boutique owner. They had two children, Salim and Naazneen, both in college. Till this time all seemed to be going well with the family. They managed their time successfully despite their many preoccupations and gave each other support and demonstrated interest in each other's doings.

But then things began to go wrong. Abdul became even more successful and began to practise in the Supreme Court. As a resident of Mumbai he had to fly out every so often and had to stay away from his family. Shernaz, too, expanded her beauty business and established a branch in Bangalore. But it did not meet with the success of the Mumbai enterprize and she began to lose money on it. She also had to cope with the law suit resulting from a consumer complaint about one of her products. In between Salim took to drugs and had to be hospitalised after an overdose. Naazneen went off to live with a businessman, not of her community or religion, whom she happened to meet. All these events which occurred in the course of three years created innumerable tensions in each of the members of the family. Abdul's health broke down. High blood pressure and a heart condition forced him to restrict his law practice and his travel. Shernaz, too, came close to a nervous breakdown. She closed down her Bangalore branch and settled the law suit and stayed put in Mumbai, in a very depressed condition. Salim was put in a detoxification centre, and there was no trace of Naazneen for a long time.

One of Abdul's clients, hearing of his family's condition advised him to try out a technique which he himself had been taught, to awaken his intuition, and had been able to use it to solve his own serious problems and take the right decisions in life.

Abdul followed his counsel and trained his wife as well to use the technique. It was so successful in solving their problems that they persuaded their son, too, to try it out. Consequently, he was able to drop his drug habit and get back on the rails.

Eventually the daughter contacted them, and she was persuaded to marry her beau with whom she was living. They too successfully employed the intuition technique to tackle any problems they faced. The package of techniques is described below.

Awakening Your Intuition

Purpose: To get a grip on your problem, its rationale and emotional implications. To find a solution to it that is satisfactory to you from all points of view. Often we tend to opt for courses of action undertaken on the basis of reason or emotion above. Intuition is a combination of reason, emotion and body wisdom that takes your whole organism's interests and capabilities into consideration. Action undertaken on the basis of intuition is thus the most ultimately rational course available.

Duration : Initially about an hour at a time, then less than 10 minutes at a time.

Posture : Any comfortable position.

Procedure

1) Sit comfortably. Close your eyes turning them slightly upward. Imagine that your mind is a room cluttered with all your problems. Sweep the room clean of the problems, dumping them into a garbage truck. **Ask Yourself:** What is wrong with my life? What is preventing me from feeling on top of the world? Don't answer. Many problems may pop into your mind. Arrange them along the wall of the room of your mind without examining them, as if they were parcels, each with a label: e.g. 'Marriage', 'Children', 'Finance', 'Job' etc - **Ask yourself:** Suppose all these problems had been solved, would I be fine? Don't answer. Either more problems will pop up, or your body will get a feeling that without these problems you will feel great. Keep arranging your problems around the room of your mind, till your body gets the feeling that you will be fine with all those problems out of the way.
2) Take up one problem for tackling by your intuition. Don't examine the problem in detail. Just recall the problem and try to perceive what feeling your body has about it. Does it feel constricted, tense, tight, choked? Be aware of the sense of discomfort the problem brings to your body, however unclear or slight it may be at the start.

3) Your mind needs a key to unlock that feeling in your body. Find a word or phrase, in English or in your own language, that fits that sense of body discomfort: "Depressing"? "Scary"? "Heavyness"? "Compression of the chest"? "Weight on the mind"? "Cold fear"? Take some time till you get an appropriate word or phrase-key.
4) Take turns at thinking of the word and getting the body's feeling of the problem and how well they fit each other. Wait till they match perfectly. You may need to shift to another word or the body feeling may alter slightly. If the latter happens, be continuously aware of the change. Keep your mind on it. Then either find a new word for it or try to fit the old one into it. When the word and feeling fit each other perfectly, stay with that feeling for a minute or so.
5) *Let us say your word-key is 'choked'*. Ask yourself: what aspect of this problem makes me choked? Stay with that question, till an answer pops up in your mind. If you get no answer pursue the problem with these questions: "What is the worst part of this situation?" "What prevents it from being resolved?" "What has to happen for me to feel better about it?"

   Never preface any question with 'Why'. Don't answer any of these questions. Wait for the feeling to arise and provide you with the answer which you can then put into words.

   If still no answer comes up ask: "How would it feel if the problem were solved". Let your body respond with the appropriate sensation. Then ask: "In what way can that happen?" Try this approach several times till you get an answer.
6) Accept whatever feeling comes up as the first step to a solution. Don't let your mind criticise or suppress

it. You don't have to believe anything. Just keep an open mind. Accept wholeheartedly the feeling the body has released about the direction of the solution to the problem. If it is not the complete solution, go through another round of questioning your mind/ body till the problem is fully unravelled.

Then proceed to the next problem you had set aside, when your body and mind are ready for it.

Expand Your Intuition

Purpose : To put your intuition powers to full use after awakening these powers within you.

Posture : Sitting.

Duration : In 10-minute segments.

Procedure

1) Close your eyes and take deep breaths, letting your body relax.
2) Consider the last 24-hours of your life. List all the decisions or choices you have made during this time. Are you happy with them? Focus on each decision at a time mentally and let your body respond with a positive or negative feeling about how wise it was. What alternatives were open to you? How does your body respond to each alternative?
3) Open your eyes. Make a list of things you think you should do in your life: "I should stop drinking", "I should get a new job", "I should learn a new skill" etc. Make the list as long as you can. Discuss it with a friend.
4) Rewrite the list, replacing the 'should' with 'could' wherever you think you can manage it. "I could give up drinking", "I could find a new job". Each time you write your sentence, consult your body feeling

about it. Does your body feel you could really do it? Or does it feel constricted, tense, resistant? If you strongly feel in body and mind you should do something, but get a negative response to being able to do it, put your intuition to work as in 'Awakening Your Intuition' to resolve the situation, or try any of the creativity techniques taught in this book.

5) Close your eyes, turn them slightly upward and imagine you are going down a spiral staircase. Count the steps as you go down, from 50, the topmost step to 1. When you reach step 1 at the bottom, imagine you are in front of a closed door with *Intuition* written on it. Open the door and go inside. What do you see inside? Look around. Take your time. Is there anything you want to bring back with you? Is there anyone in the room—a person or an animal? It may be Shakespeare, Meena Kumari or a talking parrot. He, she or it may agree to become your guide in handling your problems. Ask him/her/it for advice and it will be given.

This room is a place to which you can return anytime you want, to solve a problem or to rest for a few minutes from your cares. You can furnish the room in such a way as to make yourself comfortable in it.

Now go back. Close the *Intuition* door and go up the stairs. Whenever you have a problem go down the staircase into the *Intuition* room and discuss your problem with the personage there, to get it solved.

How to Train Your Intuition

Purpose : To train your intuition to expand your capabilities to the maximum and draw an abundance of benefits to you and those you choose to help.

Posture : Sitting comfortably.

Duration : The training programme will last for 20 days taking about an hour a day. Once the training is over, however, it will take only a few minutes to apply the skills gained each time they are needed.

Procedure

Day 1 : Sit comfortably where you will not be disturbed for an hour or so. Make sure you will not doze off to sleep if you relax very deeply. It's best if you don't rest your head anywhere and maintain your spine straight but not tense. Close your eyes and turn them upwards. Imagine you are at the top of an underground staircase. It has 100 steps, each boldly numbered. The topmost step is numbered 100, the bottommost 1. Walk down the staircase, counting each step from 100 to 1. Don't be in a hurry.

When you get off the last step you will be facing a door with an inscription on it reading *Intuition.*

Open the door and inside you will see a room with a sofa, a table, a chair, a full length mirror, a TV set and assorted furniture. On the table there is a basket of varied fruits. Take three of your favourites: say, a mango, an apple and a peach. Cut each of them with a knife into halves and observe its colours and texture. Touch it and feel its stickiness on your fingers. Smell it. Then eat it. Savour the taste. Throw the skin and seeds, if any, in the dustbin next to the table.

Now lie down on the sofa. Progressively relax all your muscles from the top of the head to your toes, first tensing them, then releasing them. When you have finished, count from 1 to 5, saying to yourself at the end of the count: "I am fully refreshed, wide awake and full of energy ". Get up from the bed, get out of the room, closing its door, and run up the 100 stairs.

Now open your eyes. Do this exercise two or three times during the day.

Day 2: Sit comfortably, as on day 1, close your eyes turning them upward, see yourself standing at the top of the same staircase as on day 1. Walk slowly down counting each step from 100 to 1, till you stand before the *Intuition* door, open it and enter your room. There is a full length mirror facing one side of the sofa, stand before it and examine your reflection in it in detail. How is your hair combed? Are you growing bald? Examine the skin of your face. Is it fresh or wrinkled? Are your eyes alert or sleepy? Is your torso muscular, elegant or sagging? Is your stomach protruding or flat? How are you dressed? Meticulously or carelessly? Are your feet bare or shod? Are your shoes polished? Are your feet well cared?

Now go to the sofa and relax yourself progressively from head to foot. Then visualise yourself in the mirror as ten years more youthful and vigorous than you saw yourself earlier. Spend some time examining your rejuvenated features. Now count from 1 to 5 and say to yourself: "I am wide awake, refreshed and fully energetic". Get out of the room, close the door and run up the staircase. Open your eyes. Do this exercise two or three times during the day.

Day 3: Sit in a chair comfortably as on previous occasion. Close your eyes and go to your underground staircase. Walk down counting the steps from 100 to 1 till you reach the bottom. Try to feel more and more relaxed each day you go down the staircase. Open the *Intuition* door and enter your room. This time you will meet there a friend, or spouse, or child—someone close to you; greet that person and watch her or him, carefully, as if you had not seen the person for a year or so. Talk to the person to your heart's content, then go to your sofa, lie down and relax your muscles as before. Feel yourself closer than ever to your friend, spouse or child in the room. Forgive any shortcomings he or she may have and accept the person fully.

Count from 1 to 5 saying to yourself: "I am fully awake, refreshed and energetic". Take your leave from your friend and, closing the door, run up the staircase. Open your eyes. Do the exercise two or three times during the day.

Day 4: Sit comfortably as on previous days, close your eyes and go back to your underground staircase. As you go down the steps counting each from 100 to 1, feel yourself relaxing progressively, sensing the relaxation in your muscles. When you reach the bottom, open the *Intuition* door and get into your room. There is another door inside the room. Open it. It leads to a meadow where you see your own house or flat where you presently live. You are seeing it from the outside; observe its colours, the door, windows, walls, balcony if any and so on. Does it look new? Is it well maintained? Or is it in disrepair? Observe every aspect of your house.

Now go to your sofa in the room. Progressively relax every muscle in your body, then visualise your home surrounded by white light. See it as a protective light that will safeguard your home and its occupants. Now let your vision dissolve. Count from 1 to 5 saying to yourself: "I am refreshed, fully awake and energetic". Close the doors of the room and run up the staircase. Open your eyes.

Do the exercise two to three times during the day.

Day 5: Sit comfortably as on previous days. Close your eyes. Go to your underground staircase. Before you start walking down say to yourself: "The deeper I go the more peaceful, relaxed I shall be. Every day in every way I get better and better at everything I do". Walk down the staircase counting the stairs from 100 to 1. Open the *Intuition* door when you reach the bottom. Cross the room and open other door leading to the meadow. All round your house now there is a beautiful garden with multicoloured flowers. A stream flows close by and birds chirp all round. You feel peaceful and at ease. Relax in the garden. Bring in anything—a book, a musical instrument, a friend—that will make you feel more at ease. Admire your house from where you are. Again let it glow in the protective white light. Stay on and enjoy your well-being for as long as you wish. Then get up, go to your sofa, relax all your muscles in one go. Again visualise the garden in the meadow and your house from the outside in detail. Count from 1 to 5 saying to yourself: "I am fully awake, refreshed and energetic". Close the doors of the room as you get out and run up the staircase. Do the experiment twice or thrice during the day.

Day 6: Sit comfortably and close your eyes. Go to the staircase and run down without counting till you reach step 50. Stop here and say to yourself: "Every day in every way I get better and better at everything I do. Positive thoughts bring me the benefits I desire". Now walk down the rest of the staircase counting from 50 to 1. Open the *Intuition* door, get into the room, open the other door. Go to the meadow. Lie down in it. Take in the sights, smells and sounds that pervade the place. Relax all your muscles and tell yourself: "When I sleep tonight I want to remember one of my dreams". Then count from 1 to 5 saying: "I now feel fully awake, refreshed and energetic". Get into the room, close the door. Leave the room by the *Intuition* door. Close it and run up the staircase. Do the experiment twice or thrice during the day. At night keep a note book by your bedside to write down any dream you may have. Write it down.

Day 7: Sit comfortably and close your eyes. Go to your staircase and run down the first 50 steps, then stop. Tell yourself: "Everyday in every way I am getting better and better at everything that I do. Positive thoughts bring me the benefits that I desire". Walk down the rest of the step till you reach the *Intuition* door. Open it, get into the room, open the other door, go out into the meadow. Lie down. Relax your muscles. Feel good about yourself and everyone else in your life. If anything bothers you, wrap up the thoughts in a parcel. Stamp it with a description like "Worry", "Problems with boss" and drop it in the stream nearby and watch it float away. Relax your muscles and say to yourself: "I want to remember a dream tonight". Count from 1 to 5 and tell yourself: "I am fully awake, refreshed and energetic". Go up the staircase, after closing the room. Open your eyes. Do the exercise two or three times during the day. Keep a notebook at your bedside to write down any dream you may recall on awakening.

Day 8: Sit comfortably and close your eyes. Run down the underground staircase till you reach step 50. Then stop. Tell yourself: "Everyday in every way I am getting better and better at everything that I do. Positive thoughts bring me the benefits that I desire". Walk down the remaining steps, counting them from 50 to 1. Get into your room and then into the meadow. Lie down and enjoy the scenery. Imagine yourself achieving some important goal in your life. See yourself in detail enjoying the fruits of that achievement. Feel good about it. Any reservations you may have, or negative thoughts, wrap them up in bundles and fling them into the stream and watch them float away. Relax your muscles and tell yourself: "I want to remember my dreams". Count from 1 to 5 saying to yourself: "I feel refreshed, fully awake and energetic". Get up and run up the staircase. Open your eyes.

Do the exercise two or three times during the day. Write down any dreams you may have, in short.

Day 9: Sit comfortably and close your eyes. Go to your staircase and run down to step 50. Stop and tell yourself: "Everyday in every way I am getting better and better at everything that I do". Then walk down counting the steps from 50 to 1. Open the *Intuition* door into the room and sit at the table. Your favourite dishes will be served to you. Eat them, enjoying everything that you eat. When you have finished, open the other door, go to the meadow and lie down. Relax your muscles. Then say to yourself "I want to remember my dreams tonight". Count from 1 to 5, saying "I am fully awake, refreshed and energetic". Go up the staircase and open your eyes. Do the exercise two or three times during the day. Write down any dream you may have.

Day 10: Sit comfortably and close your eyes. Go to your staircase and run down till step 50. Then stop and say: "Every day in every way I am getting better and better at everything that I do". Walk down the remaining steps, open the *Intuition* door, go into your room and then into the meadow. Lie down. Relax your muscles. See the hands of your watch suddenly advancing by one hour. Imagine something good happening to you in that hour: winning a lottery, getting a promotion, making a new friend, etc. Enjoy the event fully.

Say to yourself "I want to remember my dreams tonight". Count from 1 to 5 saying "I am fully awake, refreshed and energetic". Run up the staircase and open your eyes.

Do the exercise twice or thrice during the day. Write down any dreams you may have in your notebook as soon as you awake.

Day 11: Sit comfortably as always and close your eyes. Run down the underground staircase to step 25 and then stop. Say to yourself: "Every day in every way I am getting better and better at everything that I do. Positive thoughts bring me the benefits that I desire".

Then walk down the remaining steps counting them from 25 to 1. Go to your room and then to the meadow. Lie down. Try to remember the dreams you have written down the previous week. Are they pleasant or frightening? If frightening, wrap whatever frightened you in the dream and drop it into the stream. Does your dream have a theme—is it trying to tell you something? Just ponder it for a while. It may be trying to tell you to change the direction of your life, or to do something you have been resisting. Perhaps you are afraid of doing it. Wrap the fear and drop it into the stream and consider your life again rationally. Will you be taking too many risks? Let your intuition decide. If you cannot, leave it for a later time. Now relax all your muscles. Any part of your body does not work as it should? Do you have digestion problems for instance? Plan to pay a visit to all these troublesome organs, massage them, order them to release their tensions and to work efficiently again. Today begin with your muscles. Massage them. Order them to release their tiredness and tension. Count from 1 to 5. Say: "I am fully awake, refreshed and energetic". Get up and go up the staircase. Open your eyes. Do the exercise two or three times during the day.

Day 12: Sit comfortably and close your eyes. Go to step 25 of your staircase and stop. Say to yourself: "In every way I am getting better and better at everything that I do. Positive thoughts bring me the advantages and benefits that I desire". Counting the steps from 25 to 1 go to the room and the meadow and lie down.

Analyse your dreams. Do they have a common theme with a message for you? Don't try too hard to unravel them. But your intuition may give you a hint about the changes in your life the dreams may be advising. Relax your muscles and visit all your vital organs, massaging them. See your whole body enclosed in white healing light. Let this light permeate your vital organs. Order it to heal them. If any organs appear diseased or sick apply a balm to it, mentally.

Count from 1 to 5 saying: "I am now fully awake, refreshed and energetic". Run up the staircase and open your eyes. Do the experiment two to three times during the day.

Day 13: Sit comfortably and close your eyes tilting them a little upwards. As before run down to step 25 of the staircase. Say to yourself the sentences— "Everyday—" and "Positive thoughts—". Walk down the rest of the steps counting from 25 to 1.

Lie down in the meadow and examine your dreams. Consider what changes they tell you to make in your behaviour. Resolve to carry them out. Bring before you the people you dislike. Forgive them for their unpleasant traits. Any irritation that you feel, wrap it up and drop it into the stream. Count from 1 to 5 and feel alert, refreshed and energetic. Go up the staircase and open your eyes.

Do the exercise two or three times during the day.

Day 14: As on previous day work on your dreams, and get rid of your undesirable traits by dropping them into the stream. Search your life for more people you have disliked. Forgive them their unlikeable qualities. Count from 1 to 5, feeling refreshed and energetic. Surface and open your eyes.

Do the exercise twice or three times during the day.

Day 15: As before go to the meadow after following the full procedure to get there. Lie down. Relax your muscles. List all your shortcomings, wrap them up and drop them in the stream. See yourself as a new person with all your good points enhanced and your shortcomings overcome. Forgive yourself for all your past misdeeds that still bother you. Drop them all into the stream. Feel free and released. Count to 5 feeling awake, refreshed and energetic. Come up to the surface and open your eyes.

Do the exercise two or three times during the day.

Days 15 to 20: Sit comfortably and close your eyes. Run down the staircase to step 10 and stop. Tell yourself: "The lower down I go, the deeper and faster into myself I go. Every day in every way I am getting better and better at everything that I do. Positive thoughts bring me the benefits and advantages that I desire". Walk down the remaining steps counting from 10 to 1. Lie down in the meadow. Imagine you are watching a movie of the day ahead of you as you would like it to go on. Relax all your muscles. A guru whom you respect, either a saint or your boss or an elder in the family, or a famous person, appears to you in the meadow. Discuss with him or her your problems. Listen to his advice.

If you have any reservations bring them up. Ponder his advice and discuss your action plan the next day.

Count from 1 to 5. Feel wide awake, refreshed and energetic. Run up and open your eyes.

Each day do this exercise two or three times a day.

On the day after the twentieth day, sit comfortably and close your eyes tilting them upward. Run down the staircase till step 10. Then walk down counting from 10 to 1, get into your *Intuition* room and lie down either on the sofa or in the meadow and tell yourself: "Every time I snap my fingers with the intention of going to the *Intuition* room and consulting with my guru, I shall be immediately in the *Intuition* room". (From now on any time you have a problem snap your fingers and get into your *Intuition* room to solve it, with or without the help of your guru.) Now count from 1 to 5 and wake up refreshed and energetic to go about your life.

7

MASTER YOUR PERSONALITY

Solomon was a talented executive but was burdened with a serious personality drawback. He believed he had all the answers and tended to mow down any opposition to his way of doing things. In the beginning he had been lucky to have bosses who didn't care how things were done so long as they had the results they were after. He was not popular with his subordinates, but he didn't care. As he rose in his organisation, however, Solomon began to encounter problems when he had to work in teams of equals who did not take kindly to being rudely snubbed or ignored. Soon he found himself isolated and was forced to admit his weakness. A friend presented Solomon with books on interpersonal relations and teamwork. Among these he found two which changed his life. One was on Typewatching, the other on the Enneagram. They fascinated him with their possibilities and he proceeded to put their insights into practice. It wasn't long before Solomon became an ideal team member and a formidable if suave negotiator.

(A) Typewatching

Purpose : To become aware of your personality type so as to counterbalance any of its weaknesses.

Posture : Immaterial.

Duration : In conjunction with interpersonal interactions.

It has been a major concern of personnel departments, recruitment agencies, human resource development departments and corporate psychologists to obtain as perfect a fit as possible between personnel and their jobs. They have tried to achieve this through a battery of tests designed for just this purpose, with varying degrees of success.

Two psychologists, Otto Krueger and Janet Thuesen, in their seminal books *Type Talk* and *Type Talk At Work* have evolved a different approach. By enabling us to discover what is our personality type they have tried to show how to operate and thrive in any work environment or for that matter in daily life.

Typewatching, as the two psychologists term their approach, is based on the theories of the well-known psychologist Carl Jung and later developments by Katherine Briggs and her daughter Isabel Briggs Myers who evolved the now famous Myers-Briggs Type Indicator. Typewatching, too, divides people into four essential preference pairs: Extraversion (E) or Introversion (I); Sensing (S) or Intuition (N); Thinking (T) or Feeling (F); and Judging (J) or Perceiving (P). The various permutations of these preferences add up to sixteen possible combinations which in turn determine one's approach to life and work.

"The ability of some companies to survive and even thrive amid all the turmoil [of today's times] is directly linked to the degree with which employees and management communicate effectively with one another," write Krueger and Thuesen. "We're not talking necessarily about an open and frank exchange of views, or about becoming best friends with your bosses, colleagues and subordinates. We are talking about turning the many differences among us into powerful tools instead of divisive intrusions. We are talking about putting our good intentions to work in a way in which everybody wins. We are talking about Typewatching. Typewatching is constructive response to the inevitability of name-calling. Labels are perfectly natural; that's how we distinguish one thing or person from another. Typewatching is based on the notion that as long as we're going to label one another, we might as well do it as skillfully, objectively and constructively as possible. It is an organised, scientifically validated system which has been used... by individuals and organisations that want to communicate better."

To understand how Typewatching works in practice it is perhaps best to try to discover first what type one belongs to. This should be easy enough to determine through the Briggs-Myers Indicator test. For those who haven't done this test here is an effective rule of thumb: In the Extravert (E)—Introvert (I) scale extraverts gather their energy principally from external objects and events while introverts draw it mainly from within themselves. In the Sensing (S)—Intuition (N) scale the sensors gather information in a literal, sequential way while the intuitives gather it predominantly in a figurative, random way. In the Thinking (T)—Feeling (F) scale the thinkers make their decisions objectively and impersonally while the feelers do so subjectively and interpersonally. Finally in the Judging (J)—Perceiving (P) scale the judgers have a decisive and planned lifestyle while the perceivers' style is flexible and spontaneous. From the foregoing descriptions you should be able to rate yourself as an E or I, S or N, T or F, J or P.

Once you know what your preferences are (even if provisionally, in case you are not yet certain where exactly you stand) before you apply them, check the 10 commandments of Typewatching as enunciated by Krueger and Thuesen:

1) "Life tends to support our preferences, making us even more distrustful of our nonpreferences." That is, we tend to see the world in our own image or rather in the garb of our own preferences. We had better make allowances for this preferential bias.
2) "Your strength maximised becomes a liability." All exaggerated virtues become vices. Exaggerated persistence becomes stubbornness. Excessive courage becomes foolhardiness. So too with preferences.
3) "Typewatching is only a theory; it takes real life to validate it." That is, unless you apply it in practice, it has no meaning for you or those you work or live with.
4) "Typewatching is only an explanation; it's never an excuse." Like all such concepts Typewatching is an approximation of reality. It is a way to help make things work. But it is counter-productive if used to justify one's own shortcomings.
5) "The whole is greater than the sum of its parts." Typewatching is a holistic concept according to which a person is not just the sum total of his or her attributes. That is, typewatching should never be used to restrict one's own or someone else's potential for achievement.

6) "Typewatching is only one lens through which to view human personality." A living person is too complex to be captured completely by any typology however sophisticated. There are always other ways of looking at oneself which may be useful and should not be discarded because of your commitment to Typewatching.
7) "To be effective, Typewatching must begin with yourself before you apply it to others." Judge not others before you apply the same yardstick to yourself.
8) "Typewatching is easier said (or thought about) than done." Practice is the only way to use it productively.
9) "Don't blame everything on your opposite type." There are as good reasons for him or her to be what he or she is, as for you to be what you are and behave as you do. There are no right or wrong ways here, only the most productive ways of dealing with situations and one another.
10) "Typewatching can't solve everything." It's not a panacea. Nothing is. Its usefulness will depend on what you put into it.

Here, for example, is how you can use typewatching in goal setting by your family, department or company. First be aware of your own type preferences and non-preferences, as well as the preferences of your team or family members. Next be respectful of your team members' preferences. Consciously accommodating each other through mutual behavioural concessions enhances the goal setting process, making it more effective and achievable. For example, extraverts should allow others more time to think through the issues; they should listen more carefully to opposite ideas before responding; write down and submit the goals in advance for the benefit of those who would prefer to devote more time to considering them; they should rephrase team members' suggestions to ensure they have heard and understood them correctly; they shouldn't assume that the silent ones are in agreement with what they are being told: they should be invited to have their say in each instance.

The introverts should allow the extraverts to express themselves freely without later pinning them down to what they said earlier; they should share their thought processes as much as their conclusions; they shouldn't imagine their own thoughts to be too obvious or unimportant for consideration; they should express themselves more non-verbally, smiling, nodding, frowning to notify the team of their reaction.

The sensors should not reject suggestions too early in the game; they should encourage others to talk as well even if they seem to sound rather overloquacious; they should realise that the time to act will come, after adequate thought has been given to the process itself. The intuitives should give more attention to details, using a check list to keep in touch with reality, being specific in their responses as well as inviting suggestions on specific points.

The thinkers should attend to clearing inadequately expressed thoughts, remembering that working together is as important as getting the job done; they should try to foresee how the goal will affect those concerned; they should refrain from engaging in debate for the sake of ideas only—it will alienate those not so inclined.

The feelers should not mind disagreements, taking them as a personal insult, nor should they let a decision be sacrificed to harmony.

The judgers should keep their minds nonjudgemental until all ideas have been freely expressed; all goals take time to accomplish and proponents of differing ideas are not out to sabotage competing suggestions. The perceivers should not try to modify everything they encounter; they should state their opinions clearly; they shouldn't jump into an irreversible decision instantly, and should remember that even small goals are worth achieving—they are the road to big accomplishments.

Problem solving is another task whose quality can be enhanced through Typewatching. Isabel Briggs Myers developed the Z Problem Solving Model, so called because the process takes the Z-shaped route from Sensing to the Intuition mode (diagrammatically placed on its right) and then diagonally down and to the left where the Thinking mode is placed and then to Feeling, on its right. You begin in the Sensing mode by asking: "What are the facts?"; being specific and actual, listing all relevant details and being clear. You then move to Intuition by "letting your imagination run wild, brainstorming and considering various solution." On to the thinking mode, you "consider the consequences of each alternative", also "if you weren't involved, what would you suggest and what is the cause and effect of each action?" Lastly, you go into the feeling mode: "Is it something you can live with? How do you feel about the action? What hunches do you have about others' reactions?" This procedure will ensure that you don't take a lopsided approach to the problem and, more important, also ensure that the solution is acceptable to all personality Types.

Typewatching can similarly be used in conflict resolution, stress reduction, time management as in almost any other management problem or project. The crucial question is: are we willing to try it?

(B) Discover Your Secret Self

Purpose : To discover your personality traits and balance them with the opposite traits.

Posture : Immaterial.

Duration : Can be learnt in ten-minute segments, but can be practised in conjunction with interpersonal activity.

A new star has been sighted in the firmament of modern psychology. It's touted as the ultimate key for unlocking the darkest secrets of the human personality. It's the Enneagram (Greek for nine points) a nine-pointed star, each point standing for a fundamental personality type.

The personalities' characteristics are as follows:

— One is a perfectionist or reformer who is responding to a childhood of relentless criticism by trying to be faultless in whatever he undertakes. He thus adopts his critics' role, and also demands perfection from everyone else;

— Two is a giver or helper whose gifts of affection and service are aimed at earning him reciprocal recognition which he missed in early years;

— Three is a performer and motivator who won kudos in childhood for his achievements and has now come to regard his (and others') accomplishments, past and future, as the highest value in life;

— Four is a romantic individualist usually neglected in his early years and now seeking consolation in intense relationships;

— Five is the thinker and observer cultivating detachment and minimisation of needs in response to early neglect;

— Six is a fearful loyalist distrustful of everyone's motives to compensate for childhood manipulations by elders;
— Seven is an enthusiast and dilettante who remembers only happy events and envisages only happy outcomes in future, in response to a frightening past;
— Eight is a combative challenger, having had to fight overpowering personalities and now concluding that the answer to life's problems is assuming and exercising power over everyone else;
— Nine is a mediator and peacemaker, opting for peace often at any price mainly to himself, as a result of past slights.

As can be seen from the foregoing descriptions the concerned personality types are also defence mechanisms with which their possessors confront their environment.

The Enneagram has had a checkered history. Its beginnings are lost in the mists of antiquity. It was rescued from ancient Afghan Sufi practices by the Russian, George Gurdjieff, a kind of percursor of Rajneesh, who lived in the 19th century. He used the Enneagram to identify what he called the Chief Feature of his disciples, and then used various techniques to correct the personality distortions and deficiencies created by this Feature. But he didn't encourage the disciples to work on the Enneagram themselves. Consequently it was largely forgotten all over again after Gurdjieff's death, until Oscar Ichazo, a Bolivian psychiatrist, resurrected it again in the 1960s and used it to help his patients to discover their essence. Among those who attended his seminars on the Enneagram was

Claudio Naranjo, a Chilean psychiatrist and co-author with Robert Ornstein of the seminal book **On the Psychology of Meditation.**

Naranjo took the Enneagram to the United States where it was immediately adopted and adapted for their own purposes by various New Age experimenters, notably Helen Palmer, Don Richard Riso and Hameed Ali, all of whom added their own contribution to the use and interpretation of the Enneagram, which in this way became a multicultural blend of Eastern and Western insights. Charles Tart, noted author of **Altered States of Consciousness**, who studied under Naranjo, confessed: "The fact that the Enneagram of personality went beyond ordinary life, that it discussed the existential and spiritual values that could be developed if we recaptured the essential energy that was going into pathological defences against our real nature, was one of its primary attractions. It was clearly the most complex and sophisticated personality system I had ever run across. When the nature of my type was explained to me, it was one of the most insightful moments of my life. All sorts of puzzling events and reactions in my life now made excellent retrospective sense to me. Even more important, I could see the central way in which my approach to life was defective and I had a general outline of the ways to work on changing it."

In the 1990s the Stanford University Business School launched a course focused on the Enneagram entitled **Personality, Self-Awareness and Leadership.** The Calcutta Management Association runs regular courses on the Enneagram for corporate executives. They are conducted by Brother Brendan MacCarthaigh, an Irish priest who studied it under the Jesuits. He has designed the course so the participant will become aware of his potential as well as shortcomings, enabling him to "retain his energy centre" and help him acquire "the ability to see, feel and respond to the world from the position of the other eight personalities." According to a report in Newsweek, "The CIA now uses the Enneagram to help agents understand the behaviour of individual world leaders. The US Postal Service recently turned to the Enneagram to help employees resolve conflicts. Clergy from the Vatican signed up for an Enneagram seminar [in 1993, and in 1994] the First International Enneagram Conference, with 1,400 participants who came to Palo Alto, California, from as far away as Japan, was cosponsored by Stanford Medical School's department of psychiatry."

The various proponents of the Enneagram have discovered in this symbolic star a versatile aid to counselling and self-discovery. Helen Palmer, head of the Centre for Enneagram Studies, believes that in early childhood the human personality is not yet formed. It begins to be formed as a part of the person's strategy for survival. "Once personality is formed, attention becomes immersed in the preoccupations that characterise our type," she writes in **The Enneagram.** "We lose the essential childlike ability to respond to the world as it really is, and begin to become selectively sensitive to the information that supports our type's world view. We see what we need to see in order to survive and become oblivious to the rest.'

Palmer developed a technique of questioning her subjects which elicited the central preoccupations of their type. The questioning also revealed that the types are greatly influenced by the characteristics of their 'wings' as well, that is One is influenced by Two and Nine. She also discovered that some types (Two, Three and Four) are dominated by their hearts or love and compassion, others (Five, Six and Seven) by their minds, symbolising intellect and vision and the rest (Eight, Nine and One) by their bellies, that is, energy and will. It is possible to consciously cultivate one's less dominant characteristics, loosen the stranglehold of one's own type and redress the lost balance in one's personality. One has to become an 'inner observer', witnessing one's thoughts and emotions as they occur to free oneself from one's type's compulsions. "The hardest thing is to see exactly when we begin to move into these automatic behaviours characteristic of our type," Palmer has said. "It's very easy to know retrospectively what we have done. It's much harder to be aware when it's happening—to watch the habit or pattern of the emotion arise without reacting to it—or acting on it."

After identifying our type, according to Palmer, the next step is to convert our fixations into their opposite types which we have been repressing: The Ones have to learn to transform anger into acceptance and serenity; The Twos pride into humility; The Threes deceit into truth; The Fours envy into equanimity; The Fives avarice and detachment into capacity for profound relationships; The Sixes fear into faith; The Sevens gluttony into moderation; The Eights control into tenderness; The Nines laziness into action.

"When you find yourself moving into anger or fear or pride or lust," Palmer has said, "the first step is just to be mindful, to observe what is happening in the moment and to shift attention to the neutral place in the belly. You follow your breath down and in. Then you simply wait, so that your energy does not go out reactively and create its inevitable backlash consequences. At the very least you convert the negative energy into a neutral place, which allows you to more easily see someone else's point of view. Eventually, when you maintain that neutrality under pressure, an experience of essence can arise."

Don Richard Riso, head of the consulting firm Personality Types, became interested in the Enneagram when he was studying to be a Jesuit priest in Toronto, Canada. According to Tony Schwartz, author of **What Really Matters,** and researcher of New Age practices, "Riso's key contribution has been to evolve a highly sophisticated map of levels of psychological development for each personality type, from the most pathological to the most healthy." For example, in Riso's scheme there is a direction of integration and a direction of disintegration for each personality type. The direction of integration is from One to Seven to Five to Eight to Two to Four to One; and from Nine to Three to Six to Nine. The direction of disintegration is exactly the reverse in each case. "We are often tempted to move in our Direction of Disintegration because the normal and neurotic conflicts we get into impel us to find a quick solution to our emotional needs," Riso writes. "The process of integration is never ending: the Enneagram is as open ended as human nature itself. We are able to grow constantly in an upward spiral of self-transformation without ever reaching a final point of perfection or complete wholeness... [These] are ideals which beckon us onward: they are not states we can ever fully attain."

Hameed Ali, a Kuwaiti writing as A. H. Almas, believes that modern society has created an empty self designed to hunger for anything consumable, including knowledge, status, power, *et al.* They bury into forgetfulness our qualities of essence: love, strength, will, joy, understanding, compassion, awareness, clarity, truth, value, pleasure, consciousness. These can be uncovered and recovered by asking ourselves questions like: What stops me from being here and now? What am I experiencing now? What pattern is repeated over and over again in my life? Who do I take myself to be now? What makes me need to avoid emptiness? The Enneagram is useful in answering some of these questions.

Despite the promise of the Enneagram it is important to remember that it has never been scientifically tested and validated. Meanwhile it can at least serve as a refined guide to the personality—as refined as your ingenuity can make it.

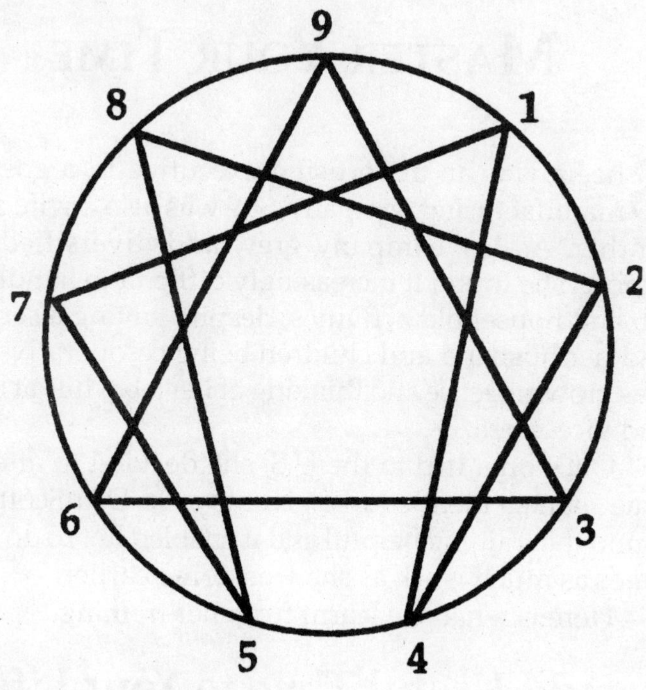

8

MASTER YOUR TIME

Sheela was an advertising executive in a garment manufacturing company. She was also a wife and a mother. As her company grew and diversified into exports she found it increasingly difficult to handle her job and household activities, despite having a servant, and her husband and children being co-operative. She was growing tense and thinking of her job while at home and vice-versa.

Once on a trip to the U.S. she decided to attend a time management course given by Dr. Dru Scott. She found the training helpful and it enabled her to do three times as much work as she was doing earlier.

Here is what she learnt from her training.

Add Useful Time to Your Life

Purpose : To make maximum productive use of the time available to you.
Posture : Immaterial
Duration : In conjunction with the day's activities.

ocedure

[T]his time management is based on four fundamental rules.

1) It is people-oriented, not activity-oriented.
2) It is based not on rigid rules but on life styles.
3) It emphasises information as well as motivation.
4) It is flexible enough to be applicable to anyone.

You should begin by changing some of your attitudes to time. If you have the tendency to wait for when you will have more time to do a job, begin by accepting the reality of the 24 hour day. You cannot stretch time. But you can use this moment more productively.

Don't be bothered if someone else's time management does not work for you. Find out what works for you best and adopt it as your technique.

If you make time schedules and then misplace them, or for some other reason are unable to carry them out, try to discover how you feel about these schedules. Do you impose them on yourself against your better judgement. Do they make you feel uncomfortable? Why? Could you reward yourself in some way for sticking to these schedules? Would any alteration in them make them more attractive. For example, by interspersing the item in your schedule with something you love to do.

Keep trying out new ideas—many of them will come to you from this chapter itself.

Is your life a mess because others around you are disorganised? Don't depend on them. Take the initiative to organise things yourself and establish some rules.

Even if you can't have everything your way you may be able to organise enough of your life to manage your time better than you are doing it today.

Learn techniques to reduce interruptions, they are great time wasters. If you think time management is a dull discipline, remember that the time you save can be put to exciting uses.

Don't wait for someone else to motivate you to save time. It is the most precious resource you have and irrecoverable when it is lost. You should need no other reason to extract the maximum profit from your time.

Are you one of those people who are always late, for every appointment and function? Find out why. Are you looking for attention? Does it give you a sense of power of having things your way? Are you trying to put off something you find hard to face? Is it because it has become a habit which you find difficult to change? Is it because you are a workaholic and try to pack more and more work into an hour, rather than concentrate on doing your work efficiently?

When you understand what your emotional needs are you may be able to satisfy them more legitimately than by mismanaging your time.

Change may appear difficult at first, until you discover its benefits in terms of a much more rewarding life style.

More tips for lateness from Dr. Dru Scott: Gear yourself to being early, work backwards, inject early excitement, concentrate on departure time, team up with the early birds.

Are You A Compulsive Time Waster?

Try to find out why. Is it because you fear to do things badly, that it seems preferable not to do them at all? Realise the untenability of such an attitude. Determine what standards are expected of you and find out how you can achieve them without excessive effort. Excessive effort implies an inefficient way of doing things. Observe how others do the same things more easily and in less time.

Make a list of the good habits you learnt in childhood and a list of the bad ones. Think of how you can reinforce the efficient habits and how you can break the inefficient ones. Habits are established through repetition, they are broken by stopping them. Consciously adopt a new habit in place of the old one, like getting up at an earlier time and rewarding yourself in some way when you make progress in that direction and punishing yourself if you fall back into the old habit —by depriving yourself of something you value.

Develop your own style of time mastery. Your style is the way you have designed your life. Any design has five elements to it: 1) Order, 2) Balance, 3) Contrast, 4) Unity and 5) Harmony.

The order in your life is the way you have organised it. Think of ways to improve it so as to make things more comfortable for you. If you are not comfortable with some of the things you do, take some time to find out why. A small change can have enormous effects. Getting up 15 minutes earlier may ensure a seat in the bus to work, or breathing and thinking time at the office before you launch into your work. Try to think what would happen if you changed the sequence of some of the things you do during the day. You may save time and effort if you do your shopping soon after lunch near your office, than after work on the way home.

Balance is what provides you with a sense of stability. 1) Try to schedule recurring activities at regular times, so that the decision is made once and for all times, no more time is wasted every day deciding it. 2) Maintain constant touch with the important people in your life. Let these be the key elements of balance in your life.

Contrast provides for alternating opposite activities in your life: Unusual and routine work, mental and physical work, activity and rest, time alone and with others, family life and working life.

Unity provides a point of focus to all your activities. What is the ultimate purpose in your life? Are your current activities leading to it? If you scatter your activities aimlessly there will be no unity in your life and your achievements will be wasted.

Harmony is a "smooth-flowing, coordinated". life. You can achieve it by listing everything that mars or detracts from that harmony and think of ways of fitting it more snugly in your scheme of things.

Remember that you have numerous choices of action at each stage to achieve your own style of time mastery. The only restriction is your imagination. When you stop to think and plan, alternatives will come to mind.

Free Yourself from Compulsive Time Use

Examine your habitual ways of doing things. Are they the most efficient ways of doing things or employing your time? Can you drop some of them altogether without ill effect to anyone? Does *how* you do things seems more important to you than the *purpose* of doing them? Then you are probably a compulsive time user making less than fully productively use of your time. Here are the five major types of compulsive time use: 1) Hurry up, 2) Be perfect, 3) Please me, 4) Try hard and 5) Be strong.

The *Hurry Up* person is *always* in a hurry, with or without reason. (The author of this book has found it useful to do unpleasant things first and as fast as possible, and do pleasant things at leisure. Few other decisions have contributed as much to making his life pleasant and productive.) The way to break the *Hurry up* compulsive is to complete your central tasks first. Plan and evaluate your activities daily, at a regular time. Be clear about what you want to achieve before determining how to do it, when you have a spare moment, check on your remaining tasks before deciding how to use it, when you plan your day make sure that your minimum needs of excitement and stimulation are met, set several small deadlines rather than a single final one.

If you are the *Be perfect* type, here is what you should do: Restrict your perfectionism to important rather than peripheral things, handle your papers only once, as a rule, unless absolutely unavoidable, Read the headlines in the papers to determine which items to read. Don't feel that it's essential to read the whole paper only because you subscribe to it. Estimate how much time is worth investing in each activity and stick to your time frame. Every day do *something* imperfectly.

If you are the type that can't say 'no' to anyone and, therefore fall into the *Please me* category, here's what you can do. Practise in advance saying 'no' to unreasonable requests. Talk to others about your projects and objectives and asking them to do things for you.

Sort out your priorities for the day and point out to others what you have to achieve before obliging others. Do something every day that contributes even a little to your lifetime objectives. Make a list of things you should be doing in any unexpected free time so others don't but in with their own requests.

Are you the *Try Hard* type that believes nothing can be accomplished without a lot of effort? Then you are not concentrating on getting the maximum results for your effort. You should first determine the objectives of your activities. Then decide what is the easiest and effortless way of accomplishing it. What is the minimum time you can do it in? Leave the major chunks of your time for large projects. Divide these projects into smaller units and challenge yourself to complete them in the shortest possible time. Use time and labour saving devices to get your work done faster—calculators, dictaphones, PC, kitchen equipment, vaccuum cleaners etc.

The *Be Strong* types try to do everything themselves. Here is what they should do: They should reward themselves when they delegate work and get it done. They should allot time for rest and relaxation, apart from scheduling their work. They should not set unrealistic deadlines for themselves or others. Procrastinators should examine their feelings on their avoidance of work.

How to Get Organised

Make a Demands and Interruptions Chart while these occur, to determine who wastes your time.

Determine who, when and why, and how they can be avoided. Sort out your priorities and keep your system for achieving them simple. If someone makes a demand on your time consider if someone else can meet it better than you. If so, direct the request to that person.

Determine Your Objectives

Make sure you know what you are after: write a Wants Inventory frequently. Decide on your life long objectives and life style. Make your short-term objectives keeping in mind the long range ones. Work on a time scale, planning backwards from your final goal. Choose your objectives first, then your activities. Do something every day that contributes to your life time objectives and life style.

When you are overloaded divide your work into three kinds of priorities: 1) Central and Essential Concerns, 2) Secondary Matters, 3) Marginal Matters. Try to avoid or reduce drastically the marginal time consumers. The Secondary Matters need doing but don't reward your efforts proportionately. Try to find more efficient and less time consuming ways for doing them. Just to what extent do your activities contribute to your life's objectives? That will tell you how much time you spend on inessentials. Central concerns are those that you most value and want to do in your life. Essentials are those you cannot leave undone.

"Always aim essential activities towards central concerns", advises Dr. Scott. If you are not sure something is an essential activity, ask yourself "What is this contributing? What would happen if I didn't do it?" "*Knowing* what is central and essential to you is the first step in assigning priorities. Doing *central* and essential things *first* is the fastest way to put more time in your life. They *always* deserve first priority. There are very few things worth doing *perfectly*. Define what these are in your life. Invest the time you need to do *them* perfectly, " Dr. Scott emphasises.

Decision-making: Efficient decision making makes effective use of time by avoiding going over the same process all over again and getting the decision right the first time. When you have taken an important decision follows this sequence:

1) Get your objectives clear in your mind.
2) What alternatives do you have to achieve your

objectives? List as many as you can, then examine them for relative effectiveness in achieving your objective.

3) Follow the Deadline Technique with its five phases: a) Classify the objectives within a firm date, b) Give yourself a deadline to come up with all the alternatives available, c) Determine the date for taking your decision, then decide based on the relative merit of the alternatives, d) Set a date for implementing the decision. Set on it, e) Set a date for evaluating the decision for effectiveness.

Evaluate on schedule by going over your deadline timetable for future improvement of your technique.

Technique for Everyday Success

Dr. Scott offers the following daily routine:

1) Do your central and essential priorities first.
2) Group together related activities.
3) Divide big jobs into workable steps.
4) Use a timetable.
5) Concentrate on doing one thing at a time.
6) Finish the job completely.
7) Do it now

Conquer Procrastination

Dr. Scott's recipe is: "Develop positive sources of stimulation and excitement that will maintain your quota at the level that's consistently best for you". When you have a boring task you would rather not do, promise yourself that as soon as you complete it, you will reward yourself with a pleasurable activity you look forward to. That is how you "substitute positive stimulation for negative".

"Identify your early childhood's unsatisfied needs and put them to work as motivators today."

"Make central concerns and essentials attractive and appealing to you."

"Use repetition, reinforcement and reward to keep moving in the direction you want."

"For fast relief," says Dr. Scott, "Clear your mind, update your wants, add your reinforcements and rewards, and do it anyway".

In the early 1960s Mr. C. Northcote Parkinson published a book that propelled him into instant fame. In it he disclosed his discovery of a new law in personal behaviour which has since acquired a degree of celebrity equal to that of Newton's law of gravitation or Einstein's theory of relativity in physics.

Parkinson's law states that work expands so as to fill the time available for its completion. The law operates in this way: Let's say you have to write a postcard to a friend and that you have a full day to write it in. In that case the writing of the postcard will stretch out to fill the entire day. First you will probably go to the post office and buy yourself a postcard. If you already have one, you are likely to decide that it is a bit discoloured and that in any case you will need some more postcards shortly and might as well buy them now. Next you will sit down to do a draft of what you want to write. Before you actually start on the draft, you may sharpen all your pencils and open your ball-point pen to check on the refill. It's only one third full; so you dress up again and go out to buy a new refill since you wouldn't like to take a chance on it drying up in the middle of your scribbling. By the time you are back from the stationery store by the circuitous route, half a day has already gone by.

In the afternoon you take a nap, wake up in a bad mood and ruin several drafts. As evening advances you get into a panic. The postcard must go today. You discard all the drafts and write out your message to your friend directly on the postcard, fill out the address and are on your way back to the post office. It is nightfall by the time you have completed your task.

The details of how Parkinson's law works will differ from task to task and from person to person. But the essential law applies to everyone. Thus it happens that the busiest man always ends up having more time at his disposal than the idle man. In terms of hours and minutes the busy man's time is rationed, but it is this rationing that makes him value it and fill up every second with essential tasks, discarding wasteful habits. He has little time for loitering and visiting; less time for gossip and rumour and no time at all for starting late, quitting early and absenteeism. He is acutely aware that poor workmanship, poor communication and inattention to detail come costly to anyone who values his time. He avoids them like the plague.

Time management comes naturally to some people and has to be learnt consciously and carefully by others. In either case the best results, the greatest time saving takes training, just as it takes training to make one a great sportsman, with one's body movements well coordinated and well timed.

Too fast a pace destroys efficiency as surely as too slow a pace. Human beings are prone to errors and excessive speed multiplies them, requiring repetition or tasks performed haphazardly or hastily. A degree of planning, however, can combine pace with efficiency. You should first set out your priorities—which are the most urgent tasks and which are the least. That will determine the sequence in which you must have the tasks completed. Thus you can fix a deadline for each task. But some tasks will be more complicated and time-consuming than others, even when they are less urgent. They may involve various other people apart from you. Such activities have to be started earlier and given more time to mature on other people's desks if they are to be completed on time.

Such scheduling is not always easy. The most effective way of approaching it is to examine your working day regularly at the end of it and, with the benefit of hindsight, run it through your mind like a movie and shorten its footage as much as possible, cutting out the non-essential activities, the repetitions, interruptions and intrusions in your time. A daily practice with this technique will turn you into an expert time saver, leaving numerous gaps hitherto wasted, which can be profitably utilised.

Apart from organising your work, organise yourself, physically and psychologically. Ill-health can cause fatigue and tell on your performance. Get yourself a medical check-up. A simple change of diet, one extra hour of sleep could get you in much better shape than you are accustomed to.

You may find some tasks tiresome, routine and boring. Boredom, too, tells on efficiency. Intersperse the boring jobs with the interesting ones; try to make every job interesting by looking at it from a fresh angle. Try to do the routine jobs faster every time, timing them each day, attempting to break the previous day's record. Make sure the quality of work does not suffer and soon you will begin to enjoy it as you would a sporting event.

Louis B. Lundborg, former Chairman, Bank of America, writes in an article on **Managing for Tomorrow:** "The man who knows to manage his own time will usually know also the importance to his organisation of time in another sense—the thing we call timing or tempo.

"It is literally a principle of nature, I believe, that the more a man accomplishes in a day, the more he expands the capacity to do an even greater amount. Work seems to feed on itself... Completion of a tough job seems somehow to make the next one easier and so on. On the other hand, if you fuss around a task, procrastinate, worry and stew about it—try everything except doing it—it somehow dissipates your ability to get anything else done."

Here is another bit of expert advice: "The best way to 'make time' is to beat the deadlines, be ahead of the game at all times. Complete jobs as early as possible. . . regardless of deadlines. by doing so you keep the decks cleared for unanticipated assignments. The result: you are never 'too busy'.

"You'll need to use travel time for thinking, reading, getting ideas, making notes. Between the hours, put the minutes to work. In three minutes a phone call can be made or a brief note dictated. In five minutes, a newspaper or magazine scanned. In thirty seconds you can make, or obtain a decision."

Peter Drucker, too, has expatiated on how effective executives use their time. He writes, "Effectiveness is essentially a practice and, like all practices, it is unbelievably simple. There is no practice that a nine-year-old child cannot understand but every practice is very hard to acquire because the only way to acquire it is through continual practice until it becomes automatic."

Effective use of time must start by determining where one's time goes by keeping a time chart. Most of us will discover that the bulk of our time is lost when we intersperse a given activity with several others.

Effective executives, says Drucker, "do first things first, and second things not at all." They have subordinates who look after things with second and third priority and which should be delegated to them.

The criterion for determining first priority is its contribution to the organisation. "The executive who has succeeded in a new job has asked himself 'What can I contribute now?' And he came up with a new dimension, something not even mentioned in his job description."

In delegating work which he himself need not do, the executive saves time and contributes to effectiveness if he builds on the strength and competence of the subordinates. "It is the manager's job to enable people to do what they can do," says Drucker.

As an aid to time-saving, you could start an instructive hobby trying to discover how famous men and women have hoarded their precious time. Mahatma Gandhi used his train journeys in third class compartments to write letters and articles. Abraham Lincoln wrote his speeches, notes and all other ideas on presidential matters as they occurred to him on small bits of paper and stuffed them in his top hat for later consultation. John F. Kennedy studied speed-reading, a technique which enabled him to race through newspapers, books and memos at the break-neck speed of 1,500 words a minute, which is about five times the average rate of a good reader. His visitors would watch him in fascination as he read the newspapers while simultaneously carrying on a telephonic conversation with a loquacious Senator.

The study of how people organise time in their work has grown into a respectable and complex management subject. Executives and workmen have been filmed on the job as a part of time and motion studies designed to promote efficiency. The solutions recommended have ranged form painting the working rooms with cool rather than warm colours, to playing instrumental piped music into them. Most of these measures are controversial. What is not controversial is that time-saving is an art worth mastering and to the extent you master it, you will be rewarded.

9

Read Faster, Learn Better, Absorb More

Sunil was taking a degree in Commerce. Although he was intelligent, his reading was slow and he took a long time to absorb what he read. His father, who worked for a multinational company, one day told him of a week's course in speed reading his company was conducting for the employees' families, as a part of its broad based welfare programme. Would Sunil like to attend? He would and he did. In a week, his reading speed had more than trebled and his comprehension multiplied. His Commerce marks shot up and he passed in the first division. He proceeded to do his MBA in marketing, after which he got a job in a consumer product marketing Company as a team leader of a product group. He devised his own training system for his group, incorporating faster learning and better absorbing techniques which he had perfected over the years since he took his week-long course. The popularity of his course eventually prompted him to design a new course for various audiences, based on their requirements, and launch out on his own.

Sunil's techniques were drawn from world-famous methodologies devised by Evelyn Wood—who taught celebrities like actor Charlton Heston, sportsman Joe Namath and Indira Gandhi—Tony Buzan, who conducted a TV programme on BBC, and various other innovators.

Here is the substance of the course package:

High Performance Reading

Purpose : To enable you to read better, absorb difficult texts, recall what you have read and use what you have absorbed in exams or any other purpose.

Duration : In 10-minute segments for as long as you find it necessary.

Procedure

1) The average reading habit is of about 250 words per minute. Anyone who reads at this speed can multiply it to 1,500 to 2,500 wpm, with corresponding increase in comprehension. This is not skimming but actual reading for full absorption of information and ideas contained in the text. The principal reasons why we read slower than we must is that we read word by word, instead of sentence by sentence, backtrack over the same words repeatedly as we proceed, sub-vocalise—that is, move our vocal chords while reading, instead of reading really silently.

   All these habits can be broken at one stroke with a simple technique. Run your forefinger under the line as you read it. You may resist this procedure, since as a child you may have been taught not to do it.

But modern research shows it is the best way to increase your reading speed.

2) Before you practise the new technique find out your present reading speed. Pick one of the chapters of this book which you have not read so far. Time yourself and read a few paragraphs. Note the time taken. Count the number of words in one line, and the number of lines you have read. Use this formula to obtain your reading speed: wpm (speed in words per minute) = number of lines read × average number of words per line divided by number of minutes taken to read those lines.

$$= \frac{\quad \times \quad}{\qquad} =$$

3) Practise running your finger, without reading, under the lines of the chapter as fast as you can. Do it for the full chapter.

4) Instead of your finger, try running a pencil under the lines. Is it more comfortable? If so, use it. Otherwise use your finger. Do not be deceived by the illusion that running your finger under the lines will slow you down. Most people think they read faster than they really do.

5) Now time yourself again and read the subsequent few paragraphs running your finger or pencil under the lines. Don't bother about comprehension but try to pick the meaning of full groups of words, sentences or lines. Check your speed.

6) Practise everyday for 5 to 10 minutes at a time, at least once or twice a day.

7) Try to absorb more than one line at a time. Sometimes the full idea of a paragraph is in the first sentence. The subsequent sentences are merely an explanation of that idea, which you may have already understood.

8) Try reading a full paragraph at a time as you run the finger diagonally from top left to the bottom right of the paragraph. High speed forces you to concentrate and increases your comprehension. But it tires you less, because unnecessary eye movements are avoided.

9) Practise turning the pages of a chapter at the rate of 2 seconds per page, running your eyes rapidly down the page.

10) Read as fast you can without bothering about comprehension for one minute.

11) (a) Read as fast you can with an eye for comprehension, trying to take in as much as you can without losing speed. Check your speed.

    (b) Keep reading. Try to read at 100 wpm faster than in (a) for one minute.

    (c) Keep reading. Try to reed at 100 wpm faster than in (b) for one minute.

    (d) Keep increasing your speed in this fashion for every subsequent minute.

12) Check your speed for a full chapter.

13) Pick an easy book you are interested in. Begin at the top of a chapter. Imagine you were reading at the rate of 2,000 wpm. Where would you reach at the end of 5 minutes? Mark the place. Read the portion *at least* at 2,000 wpm. Re-read the same portion in 4 minutes. Re-read it in 3 minutes, and then in 2 minutes. Read on from the mark for five minutes for maximum comprehension, at your maximum speed. Check your speed.

14) Practise reading at 2,000 wpm for five minutes at a time turning the pages as fast as you can using your finger diagonally down the page. Check

your comprehension. What is conveyed in the paragraphs you have read? Practise as often as you can. Make a chart of your reading speed and plot your speed on it day after day, week after week.

How to Increase Comprehension

1) Try to get a full paragraph's idea as you speed-read, at one glance. Don't slow down. Use your finger diagonally.
2) Determine what you want to get out of what you are reading. If you need only the broad ideas you can read very fast. If any idea is unfamiliar and needs explanation, re-read the paragraph for supporting arguments.
3) Use your speed reading to improve your vocabulary. You may not know a word in a paragraph. But while speed reading you pick up the meaning from the cluster of sentences and the word's meaning will often become clear without having to check the dictionary, from its context.

How to Improve Recall

When you have speed read a chapter, write down its main idea in two or three words. For example, this chapter's main idea is 'Multiply reading speed, comprehension, recall'. Then write: Who, What, Why, When, Where, How and try to answer these questions in one word summaries and plot the chapter as a map.

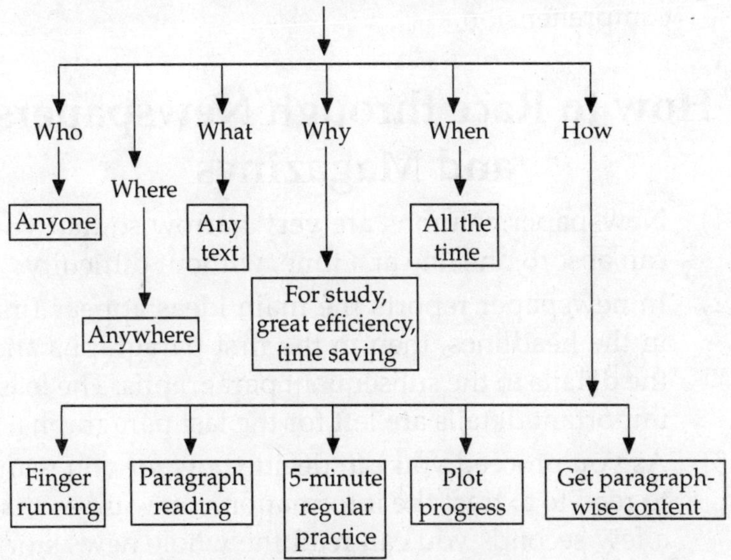

This map of central idea and attendant details will be your recall pattern to trigger your memory when you come back to it.

Make Difficult Reading Easy

1) Preview the text. Read contents, page, the blurb, the introduction. Determine what you want to get out of the text. Do the chapters have a summary? Read the first and last paragraph of each chapter. Is the book summed up at the end? Look at the charts and diagrams. By reading all these you will get a good idea of what it is about and how much you need from it.
2) Race through the book at several times your top speed. At this speed, the main argument of the book will roll into your mind effortlessly.

3) Make a recall pattern.
4) Read the book at top speed for maximum comprehension.

How to Race through Newspapers and Magazines

1) Newspaper columns are very narrow so that you can absorb one line at a time, without difficulty.
2) In newspaper reports the main ideas appear first in the headlines, then in the first paragraphs and the details in the subsequent paragraphs. The least important details are left for the last paragraphs.
3) As you proceed you can decide how far you want to read to extract the information you want so that a few seconds you can read the whole news story with full comprehension.
4) Magazine articles are somewhat different. Here use the preview-read-recall pattern sequence to extract the maximum utility out of a magazine article. That is, read the first paragraph, the last paragraph, the subheadings, if any, speed read several times at your top speed, then speed read with your finger moving diagonally down each paragraph, and finally write the main idea with its attendant details in map form which we have termed recall pattern.

How to Study Better

1) Do a preview of the text.
2) Analyse the structure.
3) Speed read at hyper top speed.
4) Write a recall pattern.

5) Review in as much detail as you can, adding to the recall pattern.
6) Review your recall pattern and ponder it, carefully considering its implications.
7) Re-read, adjusting your speed to subject-matter, for maximum comprehension.
8) Continue to add to your recall pattern and reflect on its issues.
9) Recall, without looking, the recall pattern reconstructing the information you have been absorbing.

How to Extract the Most from Lectures

1) Prelisten instead of previewing. That is, find out about the lecturer and his ideas on the subject before you attend the lecture, if possible.
2) Listen for ideas, rather than to the words. Write your recall pattern as you go along.
3) Integrate your experience by reflecting on the lecture, talking to other listeners and adding to the recall pattern.
4) Review the recall pattern frequently, for a few minutes for permanent recall.

How to Excel in Exams

Have you ever wondered why less intelligent and studious students do better than you in exams? Have you been frustrated by your lack of concentration? Frustrated by the amount of time you take to memorise concepts, formulas, facts, dates? Do you think you do less well than you should in your studies?

Here we present various psychological techniques discovered by recent research which should enable you to get the best results from your studies. They should also make your studies more enjoyable, efficient and productive.

Most exams are tests of how much material you have absorbed, and how much you can recall and express in a given time. They are, therefore, mainly memory tests. Memory is not directly related to intelligence. Success in remembering study material or anything else depends on interest, attention and persistence, apart from intelligence. To understand under what conditions you remember best, it is helpful to understand what makes you forget. There are five main causes of forgetting:

One: When something makes a weak impression on your mind you tend to forget it. This may be because you are not sufficiently attentive or interested or too many distractions or preoccupations crowd your mind at the same time.

Two: You may forget something when it does not come back to your attention repeatedly. Like the name of someone to whom you are introduced but have no occasion to meet again.

Three: When too many experiences crowd the mind at the same time, they interfere with each other and you tend to forget them.

Four: You sometimes forget something when your unconscious mind wants to forget it, even if your conscious mind wants to remember it. For example, when you are studying against your will, you study only because you are under compulsion to do so, while you are actually more interested in some other subject or activity.

Five: When the brain's functioning is impaired by drugs, drink, alcohol, shock or old age, you experience memory loss.

You can counter the first four causes of forgetting by using the following techniques. The first cause—a weak impression on your mind by whatever you are studying—is actually a lack of concentration. The more concentration you bring to your studies the stronger impression it creates on your mind and the longer you remember the material. Lack of concentration is caused by the habit of day-dreaming, lack of interest in the subject, too little or too much muscular tension, worry or emotional conflict, which distracts you from what you are doing.

To form and strengthen the habit of concentration you should:

1) Pull back your attention when it wanders away from the subject.
2) Strengthen your interest in the subject by careful suggestions to your mind when your body is relaxed. This can be done every morning as soon as you wake up.

Sit in a chair or lie down on your bed comfortably, take three deep breaths and relax all your muscles progressively from head to foot, then count backwards from 100 to 1 with your eyes shut. If you lose count in between start again anywhere and proceed. By the time you reach *one,* you should be well relaxed and your mind should be receptive to your suggestions. Now tell yourself that every day your interest in the subject will increase, and that it will help you get better results and achieve a brilliant career.

3) Tense your muscles a little, but not too much, as you work.
4) Try to find a solution to your emotional problems

that bother you, by seeking counsel from parents or helpful teachers. Many teachers will be happy and willing to listen to you sympathetically and offer you advice. Most people feel flattered when you go to them for advice and your teachers are no exceptions. But make sure the advice is suited to your needs.

To deal with the second cause of forgetting—lack of renewed impressions on the brain—here are some practical suggestions which will help you refresh your memory of what you have been studying.

1) Try to understand first what you are repeating.
2) Repeat the lesson for a few minutes a day, every day; rather than over a long period and only once or twice a week. Frequency improves recall.
3) Don't just read and re-read. Read first, then close the book and try to repeat aloud from memory what you first read.
4) Don't repeat something until you know it well. Repeating what you haven't quite mastered is less effective in ingraining it in your mind.
5) Don't break up your material into too small bits and pieces while learning it. Learn the full lesson at a stretch, whether an experiment in physics, a reaction in chemistry, the description of a battle or a period in history.
6) Improve your confidence to remember what you repeat by doing the exercise of counting from 100 to 1 and suggesting to yourself, when you are relaxed, that your confidence and memory are improving.
7) Have a fixed place to study every day, if possible.
8) Research shows that you remember an uncompleted task better than a completed task if you don't have

much interest in the subject. If that is your problem, leave off the repetition just a little before you come to the end of the subject matter and take it up next time. But if you are greatly interested in the subject, rather than in mastering it only because it is part of your curriculum, then complete that portion you happen to be studying before shifting to another subject or topic.

9) See if you can arrange a contrast between what you are studying and the place you are studying it in. If what you are studying is interesting, your study place should be dull. If what you are studying is uninteresting, the place should be bright, but not distracting. Contrast aids recall.

You may not be able to follow all these suggestions we have given you, but each will help you a little to improve your performance.

The third reason why you forget is because other experiences interfere with what you are trying to learn.

You forget more when you study similar kinds of material one after another, than when you alternate dissimilar subjects for study. You can forget as a result of something that bothers you before as well as after you study.

Here are some practical suggestions to help you deal with interference and distraction before or after your studies.

1) You will remember more if you go to sleep at night immediately after you study. Don't play a game of cards, or watch TV, or engage in after-dinner conversation between your studies and sleep.
2) Revise what you studied at night immediately on waking up, before other activities erase their impression on your mind.

3) Even if you can't go to sleep immediately after your studies at night, don't engage in mental work of a similar kind, like reading a book or a magazine.
4) If one technique of learning must follow another, choose a dissimilar form. Like mathematics or drawing after history.
5) Take a brief rest before taking up a similar mental activity, even if it is not connected with your studies.
6) Find as dissimilar subjects as you can find to alternate with each other when you study.

The fourth reason for forgetting, is emotional disturbance which prompts the unconscious mind to repress the memory. This may not happen often but when it does, several techniques can be used to recall a forgotten memory.

1) It may come back on its own after a while.
2) Rattle off the alphabet. One letter associated with the memory may trigger it back.
3) If you have forgotten a number or date, slowly repeat all digits from 0 to 9 till you come to the first digit of your forgotten number, which may trigger its recall.
4) Try to interpret a dream which you have had the previous night relating it to the repressed memory.
5) You may be reminded of the memory by something happening during the course of the day.
6) Sleep on it. You may remember it when you wake up.
7) Imagine repeating the situation whose details you are trying to recall.
8) Write down whatever thoughts occur to you freely until the memory comes back.
9) Try to think of an idea associated with what you have forgotten.

The suggestion we last gave you may not be useful in day-to-day studies, but only when some shock has caused the forgetting.

We now come to preparing specifically for your exams.

First: Generate an intense *interest* in your subject by talking to students who show such interest. Such interest can be infectious. Ask your teachers in the subject why they chose that subject as a career. Their reminiscences may trigger a greater interest in yourself.

Second: Make *notes* of what you read of the lectures and of what the teacher teaches in class. Write a summary either in continuous paragraphs or draw an outline, numbering each point and sub point, of what you are studying.

Third: When you prepare your notes, make sure that you understand your subject matter. Clear any difficulties with your classmates or teachers. Study little by little but frequently.

Fourth: Don't just read and reread. Read, close the book and try to recall what you just read. Use the P to U formula. This consists of the following steps:

P—Preview your subject matter and gain a broad idea of what you are going to study.

Q—Question yourself on the points which your reading should answer. That is, frame questions whose answers are contained in your material.

R—Read and try to understand.

S—Summarise the material.

T—Test yourself how well you have learnt it.

U—Use what you have already learnt, either by writing it down from memory or by applying it to the problems.

When you study something don't stop as soon as you think you know it. Keep at it for some more time till you have it on the tip of your tongue.

Revise as soon as possible after learning your material.

When you study sit in a position that is neither too comfortable nor too uncomfortable. Don't study with a stomach that is too full or empty.

Practise answering questions set in previous exams. Revise not only when your exams approach but at regular intervals as well.

Face the question paper with calm and confidence. Read it carefully. Find out what the examiner wants to know from your answer, then write your answer methodically, clearly, neatly. Keep your eye on the clock, dividing the time by the number of questions. Leave some time for the end to run over all your answers once.

To answer essay-type questions, you should have an outline of points in your head so you don't miss anything important. Write your answer in logical sequence. Don't use empty words unnecessary to express the ideas you are setting down on paper. Be concise in expressing your ideas, illustrating them with examples wherever possible. If you run out of time, write down only the outline of the remaining ideas, then get on to the next question.

Distinguish between the various terms which examiners favour, like comment, discuss, analyse, examine, enumerate, explain, define, etc., and tailor your answer to the examiner's requirements.

Use correct grammar, spelling and punctuation. If you are not sure of the spelling of a word, change it to a synonym or phrase meaning the same.

Be specifically careful with the opening and closing paragraphs of your answer.

Try to use one part of the question paper to help you in answering another part. For example, when you answer one question more material may come to mind vividly. Try to find out if there is any other question in the paper where you can use the material that has come to mind.

Know your subject well and be prepared for anything.

Make sure you have an extra pen, a ruler, set square, etc., which you may need to answer your paper.

Fear of Exams

When students are asked what is their main worry, they usually answer that it's passing exams. If you are one of those who are afraid of exams here are some suggestions for you: First, try to alter your attitude towards exams. They are not intended to torture you. Understand that there is no magic formula for passing them. Pre-exam anxiety can hurt your performance and reduce your marks. The best antidote is to study more efficiently, which we are going to show you shortly how to accomplish. Take your work seriously. The more seriously you take your studies, the more rewarded you will feel by your accomplishments.

You will have to face either or both of two types of exams in your scholastic career. One is the objective type, the other is the essay type.

For the objective type, follow the following suggestions:

1. Review the main ideas but also keep track of the supporting details and take note of unusual phrases, striking words, sayings, mottos and key sentences.
2. When you appear for the objective test read the

question twice and then underline the key words like *always, never, sometimes,* or *usually,* before answering the question.

3. You will save time if you answer each question as you read it. Pass over those that are difficult and those you are unsure of, and return to them later, if you have time.
4. If you can't understand the question try to rephrase it till you understand it better.
5. Fill in every blank, even those you don't know the answer to. Don't start guessing, however, until you finish the entire test.
6. If you have to complete a sentence more than one answer may be correct. So write the answer if you have a hunch about it.
7. Don't go back and change the answers you have guessed. Studies show that your first hunch is usually right.

For essay-type of tests here are some suggestions:

1) Essay-type questions are more complicated and need a different kind of preparation. When you study for an essay test, pay attention to principles, concepts and main ideas along with supporting points. Look for relationships between various topics, sections and chapters.
2) Make as complete an outline as you can of what you study. Jot down long words, phrases, quotes.
3) When you are answering the test read the questions twice. Read through all the questions. As you do this you are priming your memory to begin work.
4) When you write an answer, you may list all the facts in outline, then expand them as you go along.
5) Think as you write. Don't let your pen lead your thoughts. Stay calm and composed, and when an idea is formed, write it down.

6) Answer the questions carrying the most marks first.
7) When your answer is connected with another in the same paper, mention the connection in your answer.
8) Answer the questions you know best. Leave some space after each answer to fill in later if necessary.
9) Write the basic point first in each answer, then elaborate. For example, 'The Sino-Indian war broke out in 1962', then write why, how and as a result of what.
10) Underline key words in the question that requires you to do something like *name, list, describe, compare* and *discuss.* Then answer appropriately.
11) If you forgot something, try to bring it to mind by thinking of something it is associated with.

What to Do Before the Exam

1) How well you do in your test will depend on how well prepared you are. Cramming will help, but it will give you only short-term memory. After a few days, you will forget everything, and you may find your basic preparation for subsequent test inadequate.

   Also cramming is inefficient if you are doing it for the first time at the last minute.
2) Try to stretch your revision over several days or weeks and always review each topic soon after it is taught in class.
3) For several days before an exam try to get extra rest and relaxation. The night before the exam, be sure to get sufficient sleep.
4) Don't use drugs to keep awake, before exams. They will interfere with your brain's efficiency. Avoid medicines for cold which can bring drowsiness.

Don't overeat before a test. Going hungry is preferable.

5) If you feel very uncertain about the test, prepare a few questions very well, answering them at home within the time limit.
6) The night before the exam, don't let any activities come between your revision and sleep. Also on the day of the test, go straight from revision to the test.
7) Examine your performance in each test and try to find out with your colleagues or teachers' help, how you can do better next time.

How to Be a Better Student

Here are some suggestions to enable you to become a better student than you are at present.

First: Be clear about what your curriculum covers before you begin to study so that you don't waste time doing unnecessary work.

Second: Do some easy studying first, getting into the swing of studying before you tackle the more difficult task. Your mind is similar in this way to your muscles. It needs a warm-up period.

Third: Study your most difficult subjects while you are still fresh and, if possible, break the topics down into small, manageable units.

Fourth: Study some hours at a stretch without a break. This way you won't waste time starting and stopping again and again. Be sure, however, to pause for a few minutes every hour or so.

Fifth: When it is time to study, begin promptly. Don't allow yourself to be distracted even before you begin.

Sixth: Set up a definite schedule and don't let anything interfere with it. Do this by dividing an entire week into hour long segments and then marking off each of these for a specific activity.

Seventh: Reserve a few moments before each class period to review mentally what you have studied. Try to do this by only glancing at your notes, not reading them.

Eighth: Use a definite system of note and note-taking and try to take notes in class in outline form only. Pay full attention in class moving away from distracting colleagues.

Ninth: Make sure you take notes from your reading. Leave plenty of space in your notebook for additions and corrections.

Tenth: Write only the most important points in your notes, as well as examples in outline. Do not record long, detailed passages.

Eleventh: Record in your own words the main ideas you read about or from your teacher. They will make more sense to you later on when you reread the notes.

Twelfth: Try to solve problems by yourself, but if you are still confused, seek guidance from your teacher or colleagues.

Thirteenth: Keep a neat notebook. Disorderly notes will discourage you from studying.

Fourteenth: Keep up to date. If you leave material for the last minute you will feel over-burdened and confused, and your performance will suffer.

Fifteenth: Use good light for reading. Bad light makes students irritable and unreceptive to learning.

Sixteenth: Have a systematic plan for a brief rest after class hours. The best time for this is just after you return home from class or before dinner time.

Seventeenth: Keep mentally alert throughout the study period. Take a brisk walk, a deep breath before an open window, do some physical exercises and throw cold water on your face. A bath may also help.

Eighteenth: Ignore noise and distractions while studying. If noise bothers you and you can't do anything about it, start looking for another place to study.

Nineteenth: Practise taking timed tests at home with one ear on the bell.

Twentieth: Don't hop around the house reading here and there. Stick to your chosen place. It will establish the place habit and help your learning process.

Twentyfirst: Try to forget all personal worries during study periods. If necessary relax with the 100-to-1 count exercise and suggest to yourself that nothing will worry you now. Remember—learn to relax and relax to learn.

Twentysecond: Keep a scratch pad to write down anything that occurs to you which you must do during the day. After you note it down, forget it and get back to studies.

Twentythird: Always keep an eye on your study habits to discover where you can improve. Don't hesitate to experiment with new techniques. Try to see if you can form study circles with serious students, so that you exchange notes, and solve problems together, for a couple of hours a day. Compare their study habits with yours. Ask teachers too for suggestions.

Twentyfourth: Try to find out when you learn best. At night or in the early morning? Choose the appropriate time.

Twentyfifth: Use a straight backed chair so you are neither too uncomfortable nor too comfortable.

Twentysixth: Don't work at a task for so long that you become over-fatigued. Short breaks are better than a long break during the evening.

Twentyseventh: Consciously watch for opportunities to apply what you have learnt, whether in problem-solving or in daily discussion, even in your life.

Twentyeighth: Test yourself to see how well you are learning. Answer likely questions that may come up for the exam.

Twentyninth: Participate in class discussions. Active learning is remembered better than passive learning.

Thirtieth: Take complete rest if you feel stale, restless or irritable, once in a while.

Rapid Note Taking

Purpose : To be able to take down notes of lectures, speeches, conversation, dictation, without the need of conventional short-hand.

Duration : Ten-minute snatches of practice for as long as as needed to master the technique.

Posture : Sitting.

Procedure

1) Develop a speed shorthand by dropping most of the vowels from the words you write while taking down

notes. For example: 'Learn informal speed short-hand', according to this method will be written as 'Lrn Nfrml spd shrt-hnd'. You will notice that the short-hand sentence just written is easily decipherable. Its main advantage is that you learn it with very little practice and you can be as fast with it as with Pitman's short-hand. Sometimes silent consonants like 'h' can also be dropped. At the same time, dropping all the vowels may impair your ability to decipher what you have written down. Which is why a little practice is necessary, since we are so used to writing with all the vowels, that dropping them needs attention, and consumes a little time, but only until you get used to it.

2) Apart from dropping vowels, you can also use other time saving embellishments to aid you. Here are some examples :

   A) Just a capital t-T-unaccompanied by any other letter can represent 'the', even in the middle of a sentence;

   B) Short words like 'is' and 'of' may be fully written, to avoid confusion;

   C) Only one of double consonants need be written down—for example: 'accommodate' can be written as 'Acmdt';

   D) You can represent 't' with only a long vertical stroke, while 'l' can have a loop, 'r' need not be punctuated; it can only have a short vertical stroke;

   E) Use '&' for 'and';

   F) Develop your own abbreviations for words that in your speciality or profession, occur very frequently;

G) 'Ph' can be shortened to 'f' and 'C' and 'q' noted as 'K' when pronounced as in 'Court', but noted as 'c' when pronounced as in 'cemetery'. Start your practice by transcribing written material in your short-hand.

3) While taking notes, all the speaker's words need not be taken down. If you need only the main ideas, just a few sentences should be enough, since speakers tend to repeat themselves, and intersperse their ideas with asides, jokes and digressions. Only if you are going to make a full transcript of the talk, should all the speaker's remarks be faithfully taken down.

10

Master Your Communication

Listen, Persuade, Write, Speak more Effectively

Sumit was a shy and introspective man, the only son of a businessman. He completed his B. Com and joined his father's export firm. Less than a year after his joining, the father died and the burden of running the business fell on his shoulders. He had no problem handling the routine matters of the business, but the rapidly changing nature of the export market needed matchingly quick adaptations to new demands. The owner needed to travel extensively overseas and interact with clients worldwide. Being of a retiring nature, Sumit found these interactions difficult. Luckily his father had able lieutenants whom he could trust, and one of them advised Sumit a comprehensive course in spoken and written communication. The course helped Sumit to acquire the skills he needed and gain complete mastery over his firm's operations. The content of the course is expounded below:

The Art of Listening

Purpose : To glean important information from another party. To get to the hidden meanings of what is being said. To decipher the unconscious signals emanating from the other party's talk. To extract more information from the party than it is willing to reveal.

Duration : Can be learnt in 10 minute segments, and practised while listening to a talk or during any conversation.

Posture : Immaterial.

Procedure

1) Content vs Manner: Ignore the mannerisms and concentrate on the content of what is being said, either in a conversation or a talk. We are sometimes so absorbed in the personality of the speaker, his voice, tone and volume, vocabulary, grammar, wit, posture, that we miss the message. Arrogance can signal a lack of confidence, or lack of knowledge.

His message may not be trustworthy; you may have to check all the facts. Do not take a man's predictions at face value because they are uttered with a great show of confidence. Always check against your own experience, and if possible, question him on the rationale of his conclusions.

2) Be Receptive: Don't dismiss, even mentally, any opinion contrary to your own, or an idea which may appear absurd at first sight. Such a dismissal may cost you your alertness for subsequent information or ideas form the same interlocutor which may be valuable to you. A show of attentiveness also enhances the person's self-importance and he may part with more information than he would otherwise.

3) Prod the Speaker with Questions: It is the one kind of interruption which he will appreciate since it shows interest. Frame your questions as if you regarded him as an authority on the subject; not as if you doubted his credentials. With practice you will learn to ask questions in such a way as to veer the speaker to your point of view, without appearing to do so, and as if it was his own view originally.

4) Avoid Distractions: Take notes to keep your mind on a boring talk, or use some of the memory techniques from this book to absorb its full message. In conversation, where you cannot take notes, reframe the statements of the speaker, mentally. It is easy particularly if he is long winded, since the thinking processes are much quicker than the ability to speak.

5) Detect Hidden Meanings: Many communications, formal or informal, have an open and intended meaning as well as a hidden or unintended meaning. Getting at the hidden meaning can help you gain crucial advantage, in negotiations as well as important information you may need but is otherwise unavailable. The hidden meanings are usually signalled by words like 'no doubt', 'naturally' 'of course'. They indicate the speaker is very *uncertain* about the veracity of his own promises or statements which these phrases prefer. Phrases like 'by the way', 'incidentally', indicate that the statement they refer to are far from trivial, but on the contrary very important. When the speaker goes to great lengths to explain why he can't do something for you, it means he *can*, and will if you react strongly enough.

In any negotiation you can be sure the opposite party cannot give you any more concessions when: 1) he becomes suddenly more formal towards you; 2) becomes fidgety and distracted; 3) changes the subject; or 4) stop pressing his point of view. So long as the negotiator shows interest in the discussion, you can be sure you can persuade him to give you better terms than he has agreed to so far.

6) Content Analysis: Analyse the content of the spoken messages for veracity, purpose, the speaker's knowledge, its important or implications for you. You will be able to do this better if you study the subject before hand, at least in outline, if not in detail. Prior knowledge will enable you to pick tips and nuances that others, less knowledgeable may miss.

7) Listening is Contagious: If you are perceived as a good listener, your interlocutor will feel flattered and may be better disposed to reciprocate and listen to your point of view, too.

8) Overcome Misgivings: Reluctance to discuss a subject can be discussed by changing the subject to one of the person's interest. When he has gathered enough momentum and enthusiasm and covered his subject sufficiently, veer him back gently to the subject you want to discuss. He may be more amenable now.

How to Write Effectively

Purpose : To write clearly, interestingly, easily, persuasively and speak likewise.

Posture : Immaterial.

Duration : Can be practised in short snatches or long stretches.

Procedure

The rules of writing apply to speaking, privately or in public. According to Rudolf Flesch, they are:

1) Write and speak about people, things and facts. If you are writing about abstract ideas and concepts, illustrate with incidents, anecdotes and facts. Use vivid images. They will be remembered.
2) Use short sentences. The shorter the sentences the easier they are to understand. Sentences of 8 words or less are very easy to understand. They are still reasonably easy when they are 11 to 14 words long. The standard sentence has 17 words. Thereafter they become progressively difficult, until the 29-word or longer sentence touches the barrier of comprehension. Practise breaking up long sentences into several short and easy ones.
3) Avoid too many complex words, loaded with affixes, like dis-ap-prov-ing. Sentences carrying upto 31 per cent words with affixes are fairly easy to read, then they keep getting harder and harder to read.
4) Avoid impersonal writing. Use the personal element. Don't write: "A new synthetic substitute for wood was discovered at _______. The new product can also replace metals and plastics in various applications". Instead, write: "Scientists at _______ have discovered a new substitute for wood. Metal manufacturers have also found uses for it, and so have producers of plastic products". Less than six personal references in hundred words makes the passage hard to read and harder to recall.
5) Use active verbs, as much as you can. They make your sentences move. Too many adjectives tend to blot out action and to highlight only objects.

6) Use punctuation for pauses and stresses; periods for normal pauses between sentences; hyphen for short pauses between words (like all-too-soon) and semi-colon for shorter pauses between sentences. For longer pauses between two words use a dash; and a paragraph for long pauses between sentences. Use parentheses (or two dashes) for understressed words or sentences and italics for stressed items.

7) Recipe for readability: Make up your mind for whom you are writing; collect all the material you need; decide the structure of your writing i.e. questions-and-answer, anecdotal, a suspense story, etc; pepper your account with plenty of action and dialogue; avoid complex sentences, with "top heavy prepositions and conjunctions". Below is a list of the terms you should avoid and use their shorter substitutes instead:

encourage	:	urge
continue	:	keep up
supplement	:	add up
acquire	:	get or gain
along the lines of	:	like
as to	:	about (or leave out)
for the purpose of	:	for
for the reason that	:	since; because
in favour of	:	for, to
in order to	:	to
in accordance with	:	by, under
in the case of	:	if
in the event that	:	if
in the nature of	:	like
in the neighbourhood of	:	near

in terms of	:	in, for
on the basis of	:	by
on the grounds that	:	since
prior to	:	before
with a view to	:	to
with reference to	:	about
with regard to	:	about
with the result that	:	so that
accordingly	:	so
consequently	:	so
for this reason	:	so
furthermore	:	then
hence	:	so
in addition	:	besides, also
indeed	:	in fact
likewise	:	and, also
more specifically	:	for instance, for example
moreover	:	now, next
nevertheless	:	but, however
that is to say	:	in other words
thus	:	so
to be sure	:	of course

(Source: How To Write, Speak And Think More Effectively by Rudolf Flesch).

Readability combines ease of reading with i*nterest.* It means being pushed forward by something built into the writing. Structure of words and sentences makes for ease of reading; personal words and sentences for the forward push.

8) Revise. Shorten sentences and move them with active words. Look into your punctuation and alter it to get your rhythm right.

9) Write as if you were talking informally to your friend. Make sure you know what you are going to write about; the ideas and facts. Don't stop till you have said it all. For that you will have to organise your thoughts, notes and research, before starting to write so you don't have to pause between sentences.

Pack your writing with enough material to be interesting but not so much as to overwhelm the reader.

To be able to do all this you need practice. So practise: for a period of one month write a daily 500-word letter to anyone you feel comfortable writing to. Write about your letter-writing programme, how you are progressing, and other activities of the day. Write 500-words every day, unfailingly, without pausing to think. Try to complete your task in half-an-hour. Think of what you are going to say before you start, and make sure you have enough material to go on. Be informal. If something interesting to your reader, but unplanned, comes to mind, use it.

10) One way of interesting the reader and adding to his knowledge of a certain subject is to narrate how you developed your present expertise from your previous ignorance. This would be a personal account that would dramatise the difficulties you encountered, how you solved them. It would encourage the reader in a similar predicament to do likewise.

Here are some exercises which will help you do this:

a) Describe in about 500 words your lack of knowledge of subjects most people tend to know.
b) Narrate in about the same number of words what commonplace skills you lack.

c) What are your physical shortcomings and disabilities? Describe in 500 words or so.

d) Narrate in about 500 words or so your financial history, its successes and failures.

e) Describe in 500 words or so some of your failures in life.

11) Stick to facts, not your opinions. If you are arguing a case, do so with the help of well marshalled facts. When writing on a subject try to get hold of as many facts as you can, not only the immediately relevant ones. The apparently irrelevant facts may help you gain a better perspective and make you narrative more interesting to the reader. You may not present all the facts to the reader, but you should have them at your disposal when you start your piece. These facts can be in the form of details, specific data, figures, statistics, incident, names, addresses, biographical material, anecdotes, measurements, lists, descriptions. Get them if you don't have them. Here are some exercises to help you pay attention to facts and present them to the reader:

    a) Describe an important event in your life (first job, marriage, accident, death in the family) in as much detail as you can. Write about the weather at the time of the event, describe the expressions on the faces of the participants, the colour of their attires, the food eaten, quote what was said, in the participants' own words, etc. About 500 words.

    b) Describe in about 500 words, and in as much detail, a recent event you have attended: a seminar, a tour, a musical show, a picnic etc.

    c) Write a 500-word biographical account of a person you are very familiar with.

d) Write in 500 words or so about a recent meeting you had with a person you met for the first time in your life: a client, a new friend, a new neighbour, a new colleague.

12) If you find anything difficult to describe, use dialogue. As Rudolf Flesch puts it, "dialogue somehow has a wider reach than ordinary prose. It can and does often express the inexpressible. Use it as much as you can. Drag it in your writing with a deliberate effort".

Here are some exercises to help develop a ear for dialogue.

a) Write about a movie or TV programme you saw, using as much dialogue as possible. If you don't remember the exact words use you own, as near as possible to the original.

b) Use as much dialogue as you can to describe a recent social event.

c) Try the same technique for a conference, seminar or political meeting.

d) Write some humorous anecdotes you know, using a lot of dialogue, and making them as humorous as possible.

e) Reproduce as faithfully as possible in dialogue-form a conversation you had in the recent past.

f) Use dialogue to describe a memorable scene in a movie you saw, or in an event you witnessed.

13) Never underestimate the power of anecdotes in livening up your writing. Even asking the reader to imagine a hypothetical situation will serve your purpose in the absence of a real incident. So, record every possible anecdote germane to your subject.

All professional writers do so. They also, according to Rudolf Flesch:

a) "Save every unnecessary comma and every unnecessary *that*".
b) "Don't spell out words that can be implied". That is, they don't overexplain when the point is obvious.
c) "Use colloquial phrases to convey (their) ideas". Not always, but when using them makes their writing more memorable.
d) "Use the most expressive verbs (they) can think of. (e.g. 'He shoved a girl off a pier' ... 'They've zeroed in on 10 phenolic compounds')".
e) "Let the names, numbers, specific data and verbation quotes carry the story".

Flesch gives the writer the following additional tips to write like a professional: a) "Put each idea in a separate sentence"; b) "Start with the most general condition and end up with the most exceptional case"; c) "State the main point first"; d)"Forestall possible misunderstandings"; e)"Give illustrative examples".

Here is an exercise to help you assimilate the foregoing advice: Pick a subject of general interest on which you think you know a lot; say, politics, your favourite sport, family life, crime, etc. Then a) Write down five anecdotes to put across your view point; b) Select one of these anecdotes as the opening for your article; c) Summarise your article in a paragraph putting as much information into it as you can; d) Do the above three-stage exercise on another subject you consider yourself well versed in.

14) Here, then, are 25 rules summarising all the points made in this chapter, in Flesch's words:

1) Write about people, things and facts
2) Write as you talk (sometimes informally, sometimes not, as occasion demands)
3) Use contractions (can't, don't, etc)
4) Use the first person
5) Quote what was said
6) Quote what was written
7) Put yourself in the reader's place
8) Don't hurt the reader's feelings
9) Forestall misunderstandings
10) Don't be too brief
11) Plan a beginning, middle and end
12) Go from the rule to the exception, from the familiar to the new
13) Use short names and abbreviations
14) Use pronouns rather than repeating nouns
15) Use verbs rather than nouns
16) Use active voice and a personal subject
17) Use small, round figures
18) Start a new sentence for each new idea
19) Specify. Use illustrations, cases, examples
20) Keep your sentences short
21) Keep your paragraphs short
22) Use direct questions
23) Underline for emphasis
24) Use parentheses for casual mention
25) Make your writing interesting *to look at*.

How to Make Oral Presentations

Purpose : To speak effectively, interestingly and persuasively at small or big gatherings.

Posture : Standing or sitting depending on the situation.

Duration : The presentation can take anything from five minutes to over an hour. The time for preparation will depend on various factors, like the difficulties in handling the subject, your ability to speak easily and well, the duration of the presentation and the importance of the presentation to you.

Roughly it should take you twenty minutes to an hour to prepare the outline of your presentation, ten minutes to 30 minutes to revise it. But to practise an effective five minute speech will take a novice 30 minutes to two hours.

Procedure

Your presentation may be divided into three parts 1) Introduction; 2) Body of the presentation; and 3) Conclusion.

The introduction achieves three purposes: a) It attracts the attention of the audience; b) It involves the audience by being relevant to their needs and being perceived by them as useful in fulfilling these needs in some way; c) It proposes the central idea or purpose of the presentation.

The body of the presentation, argues your case with facts and the principles holding them together in such a way as to persuade the audience to accept your central purpose, remember it, and if necessary, act on it.

The conclusion sums up your presentation, preparing the audience for its end, reminding the audience that its needs are being fulfilled; reiterating the central idea; highlighting its main, but not subordinate, points, ending with a memorable and appropriate anecdote, quote or maxim.

Organising Your Presentation

This can be done in nine steps:

1) Know Your Audience: What are its interests, values, social status, sex, age, knowledge level? Get from your host these details and if you have a choice of subject, find out what the audience would like to hear about from you. What is the occasion on which you are speaking?

Don't forget to find out for how long you are expected to speak. Be ready with a shorter speech than is expected of you, to take care of delays.

Make sure of the physical setting where you are going to speak: the size of the room, the seating, the accoustics, whether you can use slides, a projector etc, the location, how long it will take you to reach it from wherever you are starting off, the time, is it a pre- or post-lunch or an evening function? When you have all this information you are ready to take the next step and start preparing for your speech.

2) Choice of Subject: What are the subjects you are knowledgeable about? Make a list. Would all of them interest your audience?

Narrow your focus. If you are a medical man, what aspect of your profession would interest your audience? If it is middle aged you could try: Medical effects of stress and how to cope with them.

Once you have zeroed down your topic, branch it out into subtopics: causes of stress, symptoms, most likely victims—

Decide how you can have an impact on your audience with your talk. Can you persuade it to change its life style to a more healthy one? How much does it already know about the subject? How much more does it need to know? Will it keep the audience interested?

Will it be persuaded of your point of view? Are contrary points of view foreseen and answered by the information and arguments extended? Will the audience be entertained and stimulated to remember and act on your words? Select all the material available to you to achieve the foregoing results.

3) How to Address Your Audience's Needs: Your audience may not be homogeneous. It may comprise various age groups, both sexes, diverse interests, but as human beings they have common needs like a) Comfort, b) Economic gain, c) Fulfillment of curiosity, d) Freedom from anxiety, e) Acceptance by their group, f) Security.

Your presentation should appeal to one or more of these needs. You can do so by: being authoritative in your subject, so that you gain the audience's confidence, persuading them that what you say will help solve some of their problems, giving your talk in a clear, concise, entertaining, easy to understand and memorable style.

So, ask yourself: What needs of this particular audience does my topic fulfil?

4) Catch Your Audience's Attention: Having made sure you know your audience well, walk up to it confidently and wait for it to settle down. If you start talking too soon, some of your remarks will be lost: just waiting for them to settle down will gain you attention.

Then introduce your subject, but keep it short. Don't give the audience false expectations. You can start with a striking anecdote from your experience, relevant to your subject. Stories are always interesting, but introductory stories should be short and relevant. You can also begin with a joke, if you are good at humour. A joke at your own expense will be appreciated, making the audience feel at ease. Or you can challenge the audience: 'I have a question which I wonder how many of you can answer?' But if the audience does not respond to the challenge do not make it feel small, or point at someone and try to force him or her to answer. This strategy will gain you attention but will also antagonise the people in front of you.

You can get attention by using visual aids, or playing a portion of an audio-cassette relevant to your presentation. The visual aids can be slides or even a single object you have brought with you to dramatise your speech.

To maintain the attention you have gained pepper your speech with unusual facts, more humour, vivid descriptions of personal experiences.

Change your tone, level of voice and pitch to suit the intended effect. There is nothing more boring than an hour-long monotonous discourse. Use gestures to make a point, but not so many as to distract your likeness.

5) Develop the Body of Your Speech: Your speech should be organised so that there is a coherence to it. Your arguments and facts should be interlinked. Emphasise important points by developing them at greater length and repeating them. Present your ideas beginning with the least complicated ones and proceeding to more complex ones. Also present the least controversial and most acceptable arguments first, and develop logically from there.

6) Make Your Talk Meaningful and Memorable: Your main points and arguments should be illustrated with examples from daily life so the audience can relate to them and remember them. Make as many points as possible personally applicable to your audience. Even if you are talking about a distant historical situation, remind the audience what conditions it would be facing if it lived in the times you are talking about. Be detailed and vivid in your descriptions. Collect plenty of support material which you may find useful in your presentations, if you are a regular speaker.

You can use the day's news item or an advertisement that appeared the day before if it serves your purpose and helps your group to remember your point better. Also useful: Case histories, statistics, surveys, reports, analogies. Use them to clarify and support your points.

7) Connect Your Thoughts: Don't jump from one argument to another and back again. Proceed logically by adding more arguments, or contrasting with the previous argument, or showing the result of your argument through examples, or alternating two possibilities between which you have to choose, or repeating the point to emphasise it, or using a visual aid as a signpost that you are about to conclude or to sum up.

8) Conclusion: Use an attention getter to show your audience that you are coming to the end. You can do so by pausing and repeating the theme of your lecture. Tell them, next, how it is related to them. Repeat its central purpose and the enumerate important points for easy recall.

9) Final Statement: This should be an anecdote that dramatically illustrates the point of your presentation, or a call to action summed up in a maxim or a quote.

Revise and Prepare to Present

While revising your presentation as you have written it down check the following:

Have you written it down fully, sentence by sentence, not just points or ideas?

Are you satisfied with every argument, illustration, anecdote? Ask for criticism from friends.

Does it all fit together, or does it fall apart? Can it be easily followed? Try it out at home on your family and question them for their understanding.

Does it have unity, coherence and right emphasis?

Are the main points memorable and meaningful?

What visual aids are you using? Films?, Slides?, Flip Charts?, Diagrams?, Illustrations?, Models?, Tapes?

Make sure the slide projector works before you make the presentation and that the aids are clearly visible and legible at the back.

Are you distributing handouts at the end?

Make a check list of what you are carrying so you don't forget half of them at home.

Make sure the quality of your aids does not ruin your presentation.

11

Master Your Memory

Soli was an intelligent man with a poor memory. Although a bright student, he always thought he would have scored much higher if his memory had been more reliable. He became an engineer and joined the research division of a large company. Once on a trip to UK, Soli watched a BBC programme on memory improvement by Tony Buzan. He found the programme effective and decided to read up Buzan's books, 'Use Your Perfect Memory', 'Use Both Sides of Your Brain' and 'Speed Reading', as well as works of other memory experts like Harry Lorayne. Before long he became a master of memory improvement techniques and could now boast to his friends of his ability to reel off page by page the contents of a full book. When he retired he began to conduct classes on memory improvement for the executives of his company. He was launched, at 60, into a new career. Below are the techniques developed by memory experts over the centuries, which Soli used in his own life and work.

The Roman System of Memory

Purpose : The Ancient Romans used this system to remember everything they needed to, from the points and anecdotes for a speech they had to deliver at the Senate, to their shopping lists.

Posture : Immaterial.

Duration : Variable, but can be done in ten-minute snatches.

Procedure

Let us say you want to remember your shopping list, since you have a tendency to lose it, every time you go out, in some shop or other. You may want to buy a dress for yourself, shaving cream for your husband, a toy for your small son, four kinds of vegetables for dinner, and a muffler for your father-in-law.

Now, adopting the Romans' techniques, picture the items you are planning to buy, placed in odd positions of your living room. For example, your father-in-law's muffler tied around your TV set; of the four vegetables, three tied to the blades of your ceiling fan, the fourth hanging from its centre; the rubber elephant toy for your son stuck to the centre of a wall like a hunting trophy; your husband's shaving cream emptied in a big mess all over the dining table; and your dress draped over your family deity's portrait, as if he was weaving it, no disrespect intended. Visualise this absurd picture in your mind as colourfully as possible and you will never forget it. With practice, your power of visualisation will also grow.

If your living room is small and you have a large list to remember, imagine a large room furnished with all the furniture you can imagine—chandeliers, period sofas, wall carpets, paintings, wall units, busts and sculptures in bronze and ivory, stuffed heads of lions, elephants, boars etc. Stretch your imagination to furnish an entire 10-room house. You will be able to remember an enormous list by hanging its items all over the house in as incongruous locations as possible and then taking an imaginary round of the house before going on your shopping errand, to make sure all the items are there. It is preferable to display the items in your imaginary house, from the entrance to the last room, say, the kitchen, in the sequence you plan to buy them, so the task is made simpler and nothing is overlooked in between.

You can also use this technique to remember anecdotes you plan to recount in a speech. All you have to do is place the main characters from each of your anecdotes in memorable postures and attires in the various rooms of your imaginary house. During the course of your speech take an imaginary walk into your house, introducing the characters and anecdotes they represent, to your audience.

You can pretend your speech is a guided tour of your house, which is more like a museum of ideas being presented in your speech. For example, if you are giving a speech on drug addiction, you can have the various drugs, with their labels, displayed in enormous bottles in the entrance room. Explain in your speech, what these drugs are, how they are produced, what they look like, how they are used. Then proceed to the next room where the victims of one particular drug are lodged. Describe what their habits are, how they get addicted, what their symptoms are, how they can be saved from the drugs' effects, etc, and so on. Your imagination is the only limit to what you can do with the system.

The Peg System

Purpose : To remember figures like telephone numbers as well as things like contents of a book.

Posture : Immaterial.

Duration : Less than 10 minutes per number.

Procedure

This system was first devised in 1648 by Stanislaus von Winckelmann and later developed by Dr. Richard Grey and von Feinaigle.

It consists in pegging each digit, from 0 to 9 to a consonant sound:

0 = s, z, soft c

1 = d, t, th

2 = n

3 = m

4 = r

5 = l

6 = j, sh, ch, dg, soft g

7 = k, hard c, hard g, ng, q

8 = f, ph, v

9 = b, p

You can probably commit this list to memory. Another way to remember it is with the help of the following resemblances:

1) t and d have one down stroke
2) n has 2 down strokes
3) m has 3 down strokes
4) r is the last letter of 'four'
5) Your 5 fingers with thumb out are shaped like stuck L
6) j looks like 6 seen in a mirror
7) Capital K is made up of two 7's
8) A handwritten f has two loops like 8

9) When you rotate b you get 9

10) z is the last letter of the alphabet; zero the last digit.

To remember a number you have to translate it into a word or phrase and associate it with the person connected with it. For example, let us say the local Funland's number is: 3 7 8 4 3 6. It is represented by m, k, f, r, m, j. By adding vowels in between, you invent a phrase, in this case: "Make for Maja". Maja in Hindi is 'Fun'. Visualise an advertisement of Disneyland, or a banner over the entrance of Funland with the slogan: "Make for Maja". This picture and phrase would be much easier to remember than the number. I'll explain at the end of this chapter other uses you can make of this system.

The Link System

Purpose : Same as the Roman Systems.
Posture : Immaterial.
Duration : Less than 10 minutes on an average.

Procedure

This is variation of the Roman System. Instead of imagining a house in which to hang your shopping items, hang them from different parts of your body, or from the buildings in the street in which you are shopping.

In the later case exaggerate the sizes of items you are hanging, making them almost as big as the buildings themselves.

The Number—Object System

Purpose : To remember a list of items in any required sequence.
Posture : Immaterial.
Duration : Less than 10 minutes for a list of 10 items.

Procedure

Link the 10 digits to 10 objects you think they resemble.

For example:

1 = Pencil
2 = Swan
3 = Rimless spectacle
4 = Sailing boat
5 = Hook
6 = Golf-club
7 = Flag
8 = Hourglass
9 = Tennis racquet
10 = Ten Downing Street, the British Prime Minster's Residence.

Now suppose you have 10 words to remember:

1) Calculator
2) TV Set
3) Shoe
4) Bed
5) Airplane
6) Towel
7) Ironing Board
8) Birthday
9) Planet
10) Snow

To remember these, picture mentally these words along with the objects, originally linked by their resemblance to the digits in question. For example: a pencil sticking out of a calculator, a swan on the TV set, etc. till you have snow inside 10 Downing Street, the British PM's residence. It is now easy to recall each item in any sequence desired.

You can remember an additional set of 10 items by imagining the number shaped objects tied with a bright red ribbon. So if your eleventh item is ice-cream, picture a pencil tied with a ribbon to an ice-cream. And so on.

The Rhyming System

Purpose : Remembering short lists.
Posture : Immaterial.
Duration : Less than 10 minutes.

Procedure

Here the 10 digits are linked to rhyming concrete nouns.

For example:

1 = sun
2 = loo
3 = tree
4 = door
5 = hive
6 = rigs
7 = heaven
8 = mate
9 = pine
10 = den

Now to remember a list of say:

1) Snake
2) Brake
3) Lake
4) Rose
5) Word
6) Mess
7) Cloth
8) People
9) Chapati
10) Rose

As on previous exercises picture a snake with an imprint of the sun stamped on it; a car braking in front of your loo after a smashing through your front door, etc—making it easy for you to remember a list of 10 or even 20 items.

You should select the system most appropriate to you from all the above.

How to Use the Memory Systems

You have already learnt to use the memory systems to remember all kinds of lists and telephone numbers. You can also use them to remember your appointments at any time and on any day of the week, as to remember large chunks of material, ranging from the contents of an article to those of a full book, or to recall important historical dates.

Remembering Appointments: For example, let us say you have an appointment on Saturday with your doctor at 7 p.m. (i.e. 19 hours). First assign a number to each of the days of the weak

Sunday = 1
Monday = 2
Tuesday = 3
Wednesday = 4
Thursday = 5
Friday = 6
Saturday = 7

So your appointment is at 7 1 9, that is Saturday, 19 hours. Using the peg system, translate the number into letters, that is K or g for 7, t or d for 1 and b or p for 9. So you get : k, t, p
or g, d, b
or g, t, p etc

You can select the last and make the words made out of them read GeT uP and visualise the doctor telling you to get up after examining you. Or, if you select the second set of the letters above, the phrase could be GooD Bye after you have paid the doctor.

Book or Article Contents

First you ought to know that remembering is not a substitute for understanding. Only when you have understood the contents of a book can you hope to remember them.

When you read an article or book underline a word or phrase that encapsulaters the idea contained in a particular paragraph. For example, let us say on page 17, paragraph 4, is the idea "fish are cold blooded animals".

Using the peg system to translate page 017 (just in case the book has more than 100 pages but less than 1,000) and paragraph 04, the combined number being 01704, you get the letters s or z, t or d, k or c, s or z, r, which can be made to read STeaK SiR and you can picture yourself as a waiter saying Steak Sir, to a customer in a restaurant, and serving him a large fish encased in a redish block of ice (to remind you of cold blood).

Such mental pictures are easy to remember and difficult to forget, and with practice you can remember contents of a full book, page by page, paragraph by paragraph. Try it.

Historical Dates: Imagine you have to remember the dates of the conquest of Goa by the Portuguese (1510) and its liberation by India (1961). Use the peg system: 1510 translates as t or d, l, t or d, s or z, producing the phrase TiLL we Toss. You picture the Portuguese invaders being told by the Indian ruler, "till we toss you". And 1961 translates as t or d, b or p, j or sh, t or d, producing the phrase To Be SHooeD. Picture Nehru pointing at a map of Goa and telling his generals: "To be shooed". In this way you can memorise any number of important dates.

The important fact to note in all the foregoing memory systems and their use in your life is that so far you have given little opportunity for your right brain's visualising powers to exhibit themselves. Once you do, you will find your memory expanding many times over.

12

Master Your Health and Fitness

Atul was a fitness buff. Throughout school and college he jogged, played football and cricket, did push-ups, bought a Bullworker and worked on it regularly. He also did a yoga course. He became a chartered accountant and joined an accountancy firm where he had to put in long hours of work. He lived in the suburbs of Mumbai, and commuting to town took away another three hours of his time.

He now found little time for exercise. He put on weight and went out of shape. Until he found he could take it no longer. He took stock of his free time, the time he wasted travelling, and waiting for buses and appointments, and decided to develop a fitness programme that made use of all the odds and ends of time at his disposal.

Before long he was again in the pink of health and looking as fit as ever, having shed his excess weight. To whoever complained of lack of time to do his workouts he handed out his new fitness plan. Here it is.

A Fitness Programme for the Day

Purpose : To take advantage of all usable but wasted time to improve your physical tone and general health.

Posture : Varies from exercise to exercise.

Duration : Varies from a few seconds to 10 minutes at a time. Check with your doctor, if you have high blood pressure or heart condition.

Procedure: *Morning in Bed.*

1) Don't jump out of bed as soon as you wake up. Stretch out in a leisurely fashion. First lie on your back and stretch out one side of your body, then the other. Reach out as far as you can with your arms and legs. Yawn while you stretch.
2) Flex your joints—ankles, knees, arms, wrists, fingers, toes.
3) Turn your head from side to side, slowly.
4) Flatten your soles against the mattress and press down the small of your back.
5) Lie down with a pillow placed under your shoulders so your head falls back. Now lift your head high enough to see the backs of your feet. Inhale as you let your head fall back on the mattress, and exhale while you lift it again. Begin with five head lifts and increase to 20.
6) Still lying on your back, stretch your arms on both sides. Keep them extended. Raise one leg slowly towards the ceiling, then cross it over the body, stretching the leg as close to the opposite hand as you can. Shoulders should remain firmly stuck to the mattress. Hips can roll and knees bend as much as needed. Raise the leg again and lower it against

the other leg. Repeat with other leg. Do the exercise several times. (Recommended to relieve tension and back pain as well by many doctors.)

7) Rub the soles of your feet together as you lie on your back. Rub each foot and leg as high as you can with the other foot. This will improve their circulation.
8) Rub your abdomen with the palm of either hand, starting with the navel, in everwidening circles. Then reverse direction and rub abdomen in narrowing circles. Keep your mind on the hand's movement.

The Day's Warm Up

Facial Pat: Pretend your hands are a child's nimble feet. Run them all over your face, lightly, for half a minute. You will feel invigorated.

Shake Down: Drop your hands by your sides and gently shake them out. Then shake them from your elbow, next from your shoulders. Proceed to your right foot. Shake it from your ankle, then from the knee, finally from the hip. Repeat with your left foot. The whole exercise takes 30 seconds.

Toe Touches: Spread your legs so feet are shoulder-width apart. Try to touch your left toes with your right fingers without bending your knees. Return to starting position and try to touch your right toes with your left fingers. Repeat as many times as you can for one minute.

Sky Stretches: Stand with your legs somewhat apart. Reach out to the sky with your right hand, stretching it as much as possible, then job at the sky with the left hand. Repeat several times in quick succession for a minute.

Jumping Jacks: Stand with your arms by your sides. As you raise them straight up and they meet above your head let your feet jump apart. Bring your arms back down, while jumping up and bringing your feet together. Repeat rapidly for a minute.

Marching in Place: Place feet shoulder-width apart, arms by your side. One leg at a time, raise leg from the knee but extend no higher than the hips. Then pull down —don't let it drop. Repeat with the other leg. Goose-step in this may rapidly for half a minute without straining yourself.

Push-ups: Place both hands on the floor just outside your breastline, legs straight out behind you. Keep your back in straight line with your legs—don't let your buttocks stick out, or your head hang down or your belly sag. Lower your chest, as close to the floor as possible. Raise it again. Do as many times as you can for a minute.

Deep Breathing: Lie on your back and breathe deeply for 30 seconds. As you breathe concentrate on relaxing your body. Start with your head moving on progressively down to your feet, until your body is fully relaxed.

Arm Swings: Spread your legs so feet are shoulder-width apart. Stand erect. With arms stretched outwards from your sides, fingers reaching out to opposite walls, swing as far as you can to each side. Repeat right, centre, left for a minute.

Warm Down: Standing erect, let the weight of your head lead you as you roll down vertebra by vertebra until your nose gets as close to your knees as possible. Your knees should be slightly bent, not locked. Let your arms dangle free. Roll back up, slowly. Breathe deeply. Repeat for 30 seconds.

During the Day: Standing in a Queue

Neck Tone-Up: Hold your body straight but turn your head furthest to the right and then left.

Waist Tone-Up: Keep your lower body straight. Move only your torso, waist upwards furthest to your left, then right, as if you were looking for someone.

Isometric Exercises: These are stationary exercises for improving your posture and figure. Tighten and loosen your seat muscles several times. Press your thighs together as tight as you can. Clasp your hands together in front of your chest, then press them together and try to pull them apart alternately. Clasp your hands behind your buttocks, then pull them down from your shoulders so your back aches slightly.

Wrist Twist: To improve circulation make fists, tighter, then spread your fingers wide. Stretch them apart. Rotate wrists in both directions. Flex your wrists up and down. Shake your hands out loosely. This will straighten your hands.

Standing Roll: Roll slowly forward into your toes, then back onto your heels. Roll weight onto outside of feet and curl toes inwards. Roll weight onto inside of feet and curl toes upwards. Improves feet strength and coordination.

Office Exercises

Sitting Isotonics while on Phone: With the free hand hold a heavy paper weight or phone book and lift it straight up to the ceiling, then bring it down behind your head as far as you comfortably can. Swing it out directly to the side, then make several arm circles with it first in one direction then in the other. Swing it out directly to the side, then forward to touch your chest. Slowly lower it sideways and touch the floor with it about a foot from your chair. (You should either have privacy, or your colleagues should know beforehand what you are up to. You could turn them all into fitness buffs.)

Sitting Isometrics: Tighten your seat muscles and press your knees together. Tighten your abdominal muscles and draw them in towards your spine. Press with your free arm under your desk as if trying to lift it.

Leg Extensions: While you sit, tighten your abdominals and stretch one leg at a time in front of you. In this position lift it up and down several inches. Hold on to your desk, tighten your abdominals and stretch out both legs horizontally in front of you. Make sure you hold your phone with a different hand each time, so both get the benefit of the workout.

When You have been Sitting Too Long: Walk up to the toilet and do the following exercises for a couple of minutes: Stand with your feet slightly apart, toes pointed ahead. Keep you back *straight* and heels on the floor. Lower your body about a foot bending your knees. Don't forget to keep your knees directly above your middle toes so your weight is evenly distributed.

Stand with your feet apart, knees slightly bent. Keep your abdominals tight, shift your hips first to one side, then to the other without swaying forward or backward. Improves hip flexibility.

Rotate your ankles first in one direction, then in the other. Separate and wiggle your toes, preferably after removing your shoes.

Face Tone-Up: Make a tight oval with your mouth. Try to close your lips over your teeth. Simultaneously close your eyes and raise your eye-brows. Tensing your mouth, pull the corners of your mouth into a smile with the help of your upper cheek muscles. Feel the tightness in the muscles of your face. Slowly relax. Try puffing out your cheeks like a balloon. Hold for a few seconds, then release. Combats wrinkles around the face.

Thigh-Tone: Stand a foot from a wall, feet pointing straight ahead. Slide your back down the wall until you feel a tightness about your thighs.

Pull in your abdominals and hold this position. Slide up the wall. If too hard slide down to the floor. Eventually you will be able to hold the position with your thighs parallel to the floor. Try to hold position for longer and longer periods.

While in a Car: At a signal pull in your stomach and hold till the lights turn green. Drop your head forward, then slowly roll it to the right, then back, then left, then again forward. Keep your shoulders loose. Roll your head again in the reverse direction. Keep your body still while you turn your head as far to the left as you can, then to the right. Relieves stiffness and improves circulation.

Raise your shoulders to your ears. Then release and relax them. Raise one shoulder at a time, contracting it while you relax the other. If your hands are on the steering wheel, and you are waiting for the traffic to move, rotate your shoulders in small circles, first forward then backward. Pull your shoulders back as if trying to make the shoulder blades touch each other. Hold for a while. Then release. Relieves shoulder tension.

Inhale deeply through the nose. Hold breath for a while, sticking out your tongue as far as possible—try touching your chin. (Cover your mouth with a paper or book, so people don't notice). Open your eyes as wide as possible. Exhale through an open mouth, making a ha-a sound.

In a Lift, or Waiting for It: Pull in your stomach, as if planning to touch it to your back. Press your inner thighs together. Clasp your hands in front of your chest, press them together. Then try to pull them apart. Fold your arms in front of your chest with your palms resting on forearms just above your elbows. Push. Fold your arms behind you, palms gripping the forearms.

Push your arms together then, try to pull them apart. Maintain each posture for 6 to 10 seconds.

Anytime Acupressure Massage of Hands & Feet

a) **For Headaches:** Press deeply along thumbs. If you find a sore spot massage it for a few minutes, then move on. Some headaches need pressure on the first finger and on the web between the thumb and first finger. Reputed to be good for hangovers, too!

b) **For Sore Throats and Tense Necks:** Press along bottom of thumb and along the corners of the thumb nail closest to the index finger.

c) **For Stomach Trouble:** Press area between thumb and first finger. Promote digestion by massaging this area after every meal.

d) **To Reduce Feeling of Cold:** Massage your third and fourth fingers.

e) **For General Health:** Roll a soft drink bottle on the floor with each foot in turn, exerting some pressure, from the toes to the heel.

Eye Refreshers: While sitting at a table or desk, close your eyes tightly for several seconds. As you relax your closed eyelids, rest your elbows on the table and cover both eyes completely with the palms of your hands. Put *no* pressure on the eyes. Feel the relaxation of total darkness. Take a few deep breaths, feeling your abdomen and ribs expand. As you exhale, imagine the energy vibrations from your breath go to your eye area. With your eyes thus closed and covered imagine that you are looking far into the distance—at endless green fields and blue skies.

With the eyes closed and covered, imagine in detail a scene which is at the same time pleasant, relaxing, and full of motion. For example, visualise a beach scene. Observe the waves as they break, rush in, and recede, leaving the sand a darker colour. Follow with your eyes a bright beach ball as it is tossed by some youngsters.

Eye Massage: Using the three middle fingers, press firmly along the bony ridges above and below the eyes. Move from the inner to the outer edge of the eye. You will discover points which are particularly sensitive, firm pressure on them is particularly beneficial. Your eyes will feel rested, refreshed and strengthened. Splash cold water on your eyes at least twice a day.

Temple and Shoulder Massage: Tension is relieved by massaging the forehead with the palms of your hand. Tension often accumulates at the base of the skull at the top of the spinal column.

It helps to massage the area with your finger tips. Press with finger tips along the top of the forehead, along the haritone. Massage the temples with a gentle rotating motion.

Massage the top of the shoulders. Most people store tensions there. Press for a few seconds on any tender spots. Find the small indentation in the middle and press it with a vibrating movement. Grasp the large shoulder muscles next to the neck with the opposite hand. While holding it firmly, rotate the shoulder. Work on both shoulders in the same way.

If you find any tender spot in the process of massaging, you get more effective relief if you can press down for 5 to 7 minutes.

Revitalisation Exercise: Sit or stand in a comfortable position and straighten your spine. Picture a ball of radiant energy above your head. Imagine that as you breathe deeply, you pull in this energy. Hold this radiant energy in your body as you slowly exhale, visualising all the tensions leaving your body and mind.

Most people breathe 20 to 22 times a minute. Reducing this rate will increase your energy.

General Health Visualisation: Visualise yourself healthy and strong. Frequently concentrate on this image. Picture yourself being drawn into the sun. Feel it absorb you. Think of everything that goes into your mouth as healing and strengthening.

Lying in Bed Trying to Sleep: Balloon out your abdominals as if trying to break your belt. As you do so breathe in slightly but not deeply. Hold on as long as you can. Then relax. Repeat. By the time you repeat four to five times you'll be asleep.